THE ULTIMATE MAN'S GUIDE™ TO

Internet Dating

The premier men's resource for finding, attracting, meeting and dating women online

Howard Brian Edgar, Jr.
& Howard Martin Edgar II

PURPLE BUS PUBLISHING | ALISO VIEJO

2003

Purple Bus Publishing
26895 Aliso Creek Road, Suite B483
Aliso Viejo, CA 92656-5301

The Ultimate Man's Guide™
is a trademark of H^2 Productions

©2003 by H^2 Productions. All rights reserved under International and Pan American Copyright Conventions. No part of this publication may be reproduced, stored in a retrieval system or transmitted in any form or by any means – electronic, mechanical, photocopying, recording or otherwise – without the express written permission of the publisher.

Library of Congress Control Number Data

Edgar, Jr., Howard Brian, 1950 – and Edgar II, Howard Martin, 1963 –
   The Ultimate Man's Guide™ to Internet Dating: The premier men's resource for finding, attracting, meeting and dating women online / Howard Brian Edgar, Jr., Howard Martin Edgar II.
   ISBN - 0-9741576-0-0

2003093289
CN

First Edition 2003

Cover, book and Ultimate Man's Guide™ mark designed by Gregory Trueblood

06 05 04 03   1 2 3 4 5 6 7 8 9 10

Manufactured in the United States of America

We dedicate this book to our parents, grandparents, families and friends, who always had faith in us and shared our dreams.

We dedicate it to the memory of Anna Drusilla Buksa, Howard Martin Edgar's grandmother and mentor.

We dedicate it to Jan Ho, who came to America from Vietnam at the age of 15 with nothing but the clothes on her back and the dream of freedom, inspired the best in us and demonstrated the true meaning of unconditional love.

We dedicate it to our dear friend Eli Skundric, who introduced us to our muse, Mark Victor Hansen (co-author of the Chicken Soup for the Soul books and The One-Minute Millionaire).

We dedicate it to Steven E. (Wake Up… Live the Life You Love) Schmitt, who helped us in countless ways to live the life we love.

We dedicate it to Greg Trueblood, a rare friend, talented partner and great designer.

To Rod Goodman, a fellow writer, friend and staunch supporter of the men's self-help movement.

To Greg Ashbaugh, a writer who brings great joy and insight to everyone he touches.

To Patt and Dale Jordan, who gave us oodles of moral support and encouragement.

We dedicate this book to all the wonderful women we met on the Internet, who inspired us to enlighten men around the world and help raise their consciousness about what women really want and need (with apologies to Dr. Sigmund Freud).

And we dedicate it to the millions of men who are looking to Internet dating every day in order to find the women of their dreams.

HBE & HME

What's in a Name?

On a sunny spring day in 2000, two men named Howard Edgar met through a mutual friend. They marveled over the fact that they both possessed the same rare combination of given names and surnames, and they became friends.

Though they are 13 years apart in age and were born on opposite coasts, they had much in common. Their friendship and shared experiences grew until, one day in January 2003, they decided to write a book about their collective Internet dating experiences.

This one simple idea spawned not just a single book, but a whole series of books designed to help men with such important life issues as dating, romance, relationships, divorce, raising children, managing finances, communication, health, fitness and much, much more.

And so a partnership was born. A partnership that spawned *The Ultimate Man's Guide™ to Internet Dating* and over 20 other books under The Ultimate Man's Guide trademark and the H^2 Productions banner.

*Be such a man, and live such a life,
that if every man were such as you,
and every life like yours, this earth would be
God's Paradise.*

– Phillips Brooks (1835-1893), American Minister & Poet

*The credit belongs to the man who is
actually in the arena; whose face is marred
by dust and sweat and blood; who strives
valiantly, who errs and comes short again
and again, who knows the great
enthusiasms, the great devotions, and
spends himself at a worthy cause; who at
the best knows in the end the triumph
of high achievement; and who at the worst,
if he fails, at least fails while daring greatly.*

– Theodore Roosevelt (1858-1919), 26th American President

Find great deals at: www.theultimatemansguide.com

Contents

Introduction ix

Part One: Why Internet Dating? Why You?

In the Beginning... 3
Two Guys Talking to Other Guys 5
The Dating Game Revisited 6
Finally, a Fast, Cheap Singles Bar 9
A Cornucopia of Choices 10
What Do You Really Want? 12
Ms. Right or Ms. Right Now? 16
Are You GU? 19
It's a Numbers Game 21

Part Two: The Art of Getting Noticed.

Setting Up Camp 27
Profiles in Courage 29
Keeping It Fresh 33
Win With Words of Wit and Wisdom 35

Part Three: The Ultimate Rules of Engagement.

Clicking by Clicking 39
Hide and Seek for Adults 43

Contents

Part Four: Enhance Your Image. Decode Hers.
Are You Looking at Me? 47
What You See Is Not Always What You Get 50
Playing the Internet Dating Game 51
The Women of Internet Dating 54

Part Five: Discover What You Really Want.
The Rules of Internet Dating 65
The Hits Just Keep Coming… and Coming 67

Part Six: Follow the Stars to Your Ultimate Co-Star.
Astrologically Speaking 71
Astrologically Speaking II: East Meets West 84

Part Seven: Achieve Your Ultimate Goals.
Love at First Byte 97
Is Anyone Really Having Sex on the Internet? 99

Part Eight: The Ultimate in Speed and Efficiency.
From Cyberspace to Your Place in Three Days 103

APPENDIX 107
Who Is Howard Brian Edgar, Jr.? 109
Who Is Howard Martin Edgar II? 110

Introduction

There are now 50 million men and women around the world looking for love, companionship and friendship online. Many are just considering Internet dating or completely new to cyberspace. Many have been cyber-dating for months or even years. And many have grown frustrated by their lack of success and all but given up.

Still, every day, 365 days a year, 15 million to 20 million men and women spend hours at their computers searching for friends, companions, lovers or soul mates, and hours more hoping to find just the right one to share their time and, perhaps, their life with. Most have only a vague idea of where to go or how to find what they're looking for.

But when it comes to Internet dating, you need more than just a vague idea to be successful. You need a goal, a plan of action and the right tools with which to accomplish your objective. In this book, we will lead you step-by-step to greater online dating success than you ever dreamed of – providing all the tools you need to:

- Determine your real dating needs and wants
- Build a profile of your perfect female
- Zero in on the right dating service for you
- Craft an attention-getting profile
- Use email to attract the women you want
- Read between the lines of a woman's profile
- Conduct free searches to quickly locate any kind of woman
- Understand how astrology determines your compatibility
- "Meet" hundreds of new women every week

- Find dates on short notice for any occasion
- Make better choices for long-term relationships and marriage
- Discover the woman of your dreams

You will also notice "Hot Tips" sprinkled throughout the book. These highlight some of the key points contained in our chapters. So, whether you love reading or not, you can still learn something useful about online dating.

The Ultimate Man's Guide™ to Internet Dating is your ultimate resource for online dating advice. We urge you to read it over and over to capture the valuable insights and timesaving techniques contained in these pages – and turn them into your own plan for finding the best relationship you have ever had in your life.

PART ONE:

Why Internet Dating? Why You?

"Woman gives herself as a prize to the weak and as a prop to the strong, and no man ever has what he should."

— Cesare Pavese, 1908-1950

In The Beginning...

Welcome to *The Ultimate Man's Guide™ to Internet Dating*.

Why a book about online dating? It has become an American cultural phenomenon during the last few years as dating websites suddenly doubled and tripled their memberships in the wake of the September 11, 2001 terrorist attacks. Many people who once joked about Internet dating are now doing it themselves. In fact, over 12% of the population is doing it. In case you haven't noticed, Internet dating has suddenly become respectable.

Why a book exclusively for men? Until now, there were no real male-oriented self-help books about Internet dating. Sure, there were lots of books aimed at showing you how to build a tool shed, clean a gun or swap out the guts of your toilet – typical guy stuff. But there was nothing written from the experienced male perspective to help you meet and market yourself to women online or communicate with the women who market themselves to you. In fact, there were hardly any books about the current Internet dating scene at all.

It's a cliché that most men won't stop for help with directions. Could that be why there are so few self-help books aimed at them? Just walk into any bookstore and ask for the "men's self-help or men's studies" section. One of our friends did this at several local bookstores. In every case, they looked at him as if he had a third eye. But in every case, they were easily able to point him toward the women's section.

The fact is, scant few books have been written for men about subjects such as dating, communicating with the opposite sex, choosing the right woman, having a successful relationship, raising children alone, finding true love and getting more out of sex, love, marriage and divorce. There are women's self-help books galore but precious few for men.

We want to change that. We want to empower you to gain mastery over Internet dating. We want to help you make the most of your online dating experiences so that you can find the kind of woman and relationship you really want and need.

So we decided to fill the men's self-help void. For over two years, we immersed ourselves in the new world order of Internet dating, soaking up a wide variety of experiences and, in the process, learning the tips and tricks of the trade. We did not set out to write a book. We set out to meet attractive women.

And we did. Between us, we viewed thousands of profiles, met and dated hundreds of women and interviewed hundreds more. We also talked to hundreds of men about their online and offline dating experiences. Throughout the process, we found ourselves advising our male friends and their friends simply because they asked us. They were curious about why we seemed to have a limitless supply of attractive dates for all occasions. At times, we were meeting or dating five, six or more women a week.

Our male and female friends tossed off comments about us writing a book. We turned deaf ears, at first. But, ultimately, our 92 years' combined experience as males, 65 years' experience with women and nearly 40 years' experience as writers compelled us to write this book.

Like many others before us, we were tired of singles bars and the types of women we met there. One of us had even survived two divorces (look for *The Ultimate Man's Guide™ to Surviving Divorce*) and flourished.

Friends suggested we try an online dating service. At first, we laughed. Then, after a long deliberation, we decided to go for it. That's when we discovered the amazing possibilities of the Internet.

Two Guys Talking to Other Guys

We are not doctors, psychologists or sociologists. We're not computer geeks or techies, either. We're just a couple of men who learned how to meet far more women in far less time than we ever imagined.

Like most working guys today, we have precious little time to meet females outside of work. The notion of workplace romances didn't appeal to us, either. We needed to meet women more quickly, efficiently and inexpensively than ever before.

During our research, we learned a great deal about Internet dating, both from our own experiences and the experiences of those we interviewed. We also learned a good deal about what women are looking for – and even more about ourselves.

We have already found all the pitfalls and learned how to avoid them. We have done the research and learned the angles. And what we're about to share with you can save you hundreds of hours of wasted time and lots of money.

We spent a year compiling information on Internet dating sites and the people who use them. What we learned about online dating could fill several books. But, for now, this book will provide everything you need to get started. Compared to the alternatives, Internet dating is faster and cheaper than a McDonald's value meal.

The Dating Game Revisited

Interest in dating is now at an all-time high in America. How else would you explain the rapid development and creation of so many reality-based TV dating shows? At this writing, America's TV offerings include:

Are You Hot?
Blind Date
Change of Heart
Cheaters
Date Plate
Dating by Design
Elimidate
Extreme Dating
Meet the Folks
RendezView
Star Dates
Shipmates
The Bachelor
The Bachelorette
The Fifth Wheel

And that's not a complete list. Some readers may recall a time when *The Dating Game* and the *Newlywed Game* were the only games in town.

Today, even married people are watching dating shows, if only to live vicariously through all those swinging singles soaking up their TV air time. To reach this segment of viewers more directly, TV has now given us *Married by America,* a reality show that lets the viewing audience call in and choose marriage partners for several eligible bachelors and bachelorettes.

We then look on as the couples court each other up close and personal – as roommates – until they marry. Yikes! Where will it all lead?

A more recent phenomenon is known as "speed dating." This is where groups of like-minded singles meet at a club and spend a series of five-minute interludes with each of several members of the opposite sex. The goal is to hook up with someone for a date based on your most successful five-minute meeting. Five minutes, indeed. Right now, your grandparents are shaking their heads or spinning in their graves over this.

There are still the more traditional offline dating services (some have been around since the 1970s) that offer prescreened members an online dating component for an extra $200 or so per year. But the online service is an add-on and requires a password and membership number to enter. Some offline dating services will charge you $3,000 to $5,000 or more for a three-year membership and access to their database of prescreened potential dates. It's an expensive proposition at best. And it's painfully slow to bear fruit. Despite that, we both know couples who met and married that way.

One of us joined an established, well-known national offline service for three years. But, in three years of offline dating, there were only 11 total face-to-face meetings. That's about one date every three months. On the Internet, you can expect 11 or more dates during your *first month*.

On the Internet, three years is unheard of. It's all about speed and efficiency. Even 90 days is an eternity on the Internet.

We talked to online daters who were compelled, either by success or failure, to log off for months at a time after just two or three months of active searching and dating. We're not going to kid you. Online dating takes time and work. It can wear you out, or it can exhilarate you to the point of needing a break.

What makes the non-Internet dating process so slow is that the host service acts as intermediary between you and every woman you select. When someone catches your eye or captivates you with her profile, you tell the service you want to meet her. The service sends her a snail mail message alerting her to your interest. She might respond in a few days, or weeks, or even months if she's actively dating. While all this is going on, you can wait like an expectant father or select more women in the hope that someone will respond more quickly.

Now we know why they make you sign up for three years.

Finally, a Fast, Cheap Singles Bar

The Internet is rapidly becoming the biggest singles bar of our time. But, unlike your basic singles bar, the Internet offers two stellar benefits every male will appreciate: blazing high speed and serious financial economy.

So, let's talk speed first.

Ask yourself this question: How many nights in bars would it take to meet 100 women? How about meeting 1,000 women? For most of us, we're probably talking years, possibly even decades.

One of us invested nearly three years just to meet a dozen women from an offline dating service. Compare that to what you can accomplish in cyberspace. You can "meet" 100 women in less than an hour and 1,000 women over the weekend. One of our female friends "met" 13,000 men in one year. If you count viewing someone's online profile as "meeting" them, we were "meeting" about 200 women a night during our last few months online, or about 70,000 in a year.

Better still, in a relatively small amount of time in cyberspace, you can learn more than you might on two or three dates. You can meet a woman face-to-face in as little as two or three days after the first contact if you want. In a later chapter, we'll describe the process for you and show you just how easy it can be when you're online.

The choices are yours in cyberspace. And oh, what choices await you!

A Cornucopia of Choices

With an estimated 35 million to 40 million Americans and nearly double that number worldwide now participating in online dating services, there's a veritable smorgasbord of eligible women waiting to meet you at any given moment. Match.com alone has well over 8 million members worldwide. And that's just one of dozens of dating sites growing by many thousands of members daily.

According to *People* magazine's 2003 poll of over 1,400 single men and women between the ages of 18 and 44, only 12% of women admitted to online dating versus 16% of men. If you play those percentages out to the general population and add in all the singles over the age of 44, and all the people who won't admit to anything, you get a total online dating pool of about 35 million to 40 million Americans. Whether you're looking for that one special woman, or 100 women, 35 million to 40 million is quite a pool.

We already mentioned the Internet's financial economy.

Consider that seven days a week, 24 hours a day, you can discover hundreds, even thousands, of women who might suit your fancy. And, in most cases, all it costs for 90 days worth of unlimited access is the equivalent of a single night's bar tab. For most of us, that's about $50, or a paltry 55 cents a day.

Online dating is fast and cheap. Like an amusement park thrill ride that's tailor-made for the ultimate man. And, if you play your cards right, you can have a limitless supply of day, night and weekend amusement for as long as your bank account and your stamina hold up.

This book is for all the men who deserve to have more fun and enjoyment in their lives. In our minds, that means virtually every man on the planet. This book will give you all the tools you need to turn the Internet dating scene into your own little personal cyber-playground, or help you find the love match of your life. The choice is all yours. Our goal is to help you make an informed, enlightened choice – the best choice for *you*.

So get ready. You're about to have more fun than you have ever had online. And all you need is a computer with an Internet connection and your choice of a modem, cable modem or DSL service.

So where do you start? Where are these women of the Internet? How do you find them? How do you market yourself to them? How do you attract the ones you want? How do you avoid the ones you don't want? What do you say to them? How do you romance them? And how do you get the ones you really want into your life? This book answers all these questions and more.

What Do You Really Want?

Before you fire up your Internet connection, you need to take stock. Not the Smith-Barney type of stock, but the type where you kick back with your favorite beverage and really think about the kind of woman you're looking for. Close your eyes for a moment. Make a mental picture of her. How old is she? How tall is she? What color are her hair and eyes? What kind of shape is she in? And, perhaps more important than her physical attributes, what kind of personality does she have?

Is she amazing? Is she impressive? Do you even want someone who is amazing and/or impressive? If you are like many men, you probably value intelligence, a sense of humor, good looks and romance in your potential mate.

HOT TIP NUMBER 1 – *DO detail your search down to eye and hair color, height, body type, age, astrological sign, ethnicity, income, religion, languages spoken, how far they live from your place of residence and whether they drink and smoke. This will help ensure that you find the right women for you.*

Does she have children? Do you want a ready-made family? Can she support herself and her children? Can she support you? Can she give you the time and attention you need and deserve? Can you support her and her children? What about her big slobbering dog or her three cats?

If she doesn't have children, does she want some? Is she career-minded, fun-loving, passionate, sexy, free-spirited, submissive, dominant, talkative, quiet, shy, giving, outgoing, honest, well-adjusted, creative, entrepreneurial or independent? Is she funny, serious, mature, playful, intelligent, supportive, articulate, educated, caring, kind or simple?

What do you really want? What kinds of women have you attracted in the past? What kind of women have you dated or married? Were they good for you? Did they make you happy? Did they enhance your life? Do you want that kind of woman again? Or do you want someone completely different?

Do you want an exotic Asian woman? Would you like to meet a sultry Latin-American or European? How about a blonde-haired, blue-eyed, 5'10" Nordic amazon warrior princess?

On Match.com, you can detail your search down to eye and hair color, height, body type, age, astrological sign, ethnicity, career type, income, religion, languages spoken, how far they live from your place of residence and whether they drink, smoke and have or want children. You can cast the smallest net possible or open yourself up to limitless opportunities. There are just as many search possibilities as there are people searching. It's all up to you. And how well you use the tools at your disposal.

Learn to use the tools your online dating service provides. The detailed search capabilities on Match.com can really help you cut to the chase and zero in on your preferred significant other right from the comfort of your computer chair.

Match.com lets you search using a member's online name (very few members use their real names and adopt pet names or "handles" for security reasons). But that only works if you know the online name you are looking for. If you haven't singled anyone out yet, there are broader search options. You can do a detailed search such as the one we described above.

The detailed search option lets you narrow the field virtually any way you want. If you only date blondes, you can search for only blondes. If you only date women with athletic or slender bodies, you can click the buttons to select these body types. Select other factors such as age, location, education and religion, and it's easy to see just how precise your search can be.

You can do a quick search based on age and distance from where you live. Obviously, this will give you a larger pool of females from which to choose. You can even do a keyword search that looks for certain words or phrases in a woman's profile. If you want someone who loves to travel, type "travel" into the search window. If you're looking for sex, type words such as "sex," "sexy," "curvy" or "erotic" into the search window, as many men do. If you want more immediate gratification, there's even an "Online Now" search on Match.com. This function allows you to zero in on women who are logged on to Match.com at the same moment you are.

And don't forget to search for her zodiac sign. Come on, we're serious. Astrology simply cannot be overlooked by anyone seriously interested in meeting a good match, whether it's online or offline. You will learn much more about the power of astrological connections in relationships, and how you can use them to your advantage, later in this book.

For now, start by making a list of all the physical, emotional, intellectual and spiritual qualities and values you want in a female. Add lifestyle-related qualities such as smoking, drinking, drug use, exercise, hobbies and favorite activities. When you're finished, you'll have a profile of your ideal woman. Consider her astrological sign and anything else you can learn about her chart. Are you astrologically compatible? As you will see, the answer really matters.

What if you're the kind of guy who doesn't really know what he wants until he sees it? If this is you, prepare to spend hours at surfing women's pictures and profiles. If this is you, a DSL hookup or cable modem connection (at about $50 per month) will prove invaluable. Those pictures will load at light-speed. But if you're stuck with a standard 56k modem, your search time will be many times longer. You can use this extra time to do your laundry, pay your bills, check your stocks or read the latest issue of *Men's Health* or *Maxim*. The choice is yours.

What if a woman's physical qualities don't really count for much with you and waiting for all those pictures to load is low on your priority list? What if you base everything on personality, common interests or that elusive quality known as "chemistry"? If this is you, the next section may be a bit more helpful. We'll help you ask the right questions and make the best choice for yourself.

HOT TIP NUMBER 2 – *DO list all the physical, emotional, intellectual and spiritual qualities and values you want in a female. Add lifestyle-related qualities such as smoking, drinking, drug use, exercise, hobbies and favorite activities. When you're finished, you'll have a profile of your ideal woman.*

Ms. Right or Ms. Right Now?

This is a critical distinction. Do you want companionship? Are you looking for a "steady" or a girlfriend? Do you crave a new sex partner? Or a new sex partner every week? How about a different one each night of the week and two on Saturdays? Think about it. Anything is possible on the Internet.

According to the February 2003 *People* dating survey, nearly 60% of single men and nearly 70% of single women said they were looking for *companionship*. Only 14% of women and 12% of men said they were looking for marriage. The rest just wanted something to do, someone to do it with or someone to talk to.

Be honest with yourself and the women you meet.

If you want "Ms. Right Now," try a site such as alt.com. The "alt" stands for alternative lifestyles, but it might as well stand for SEX. This is the place to go when you really want to "hook up." Sister site adultfriendfinder.com is a slightly tamer version with over 20 million members. With either site, SEX *is first* on the menu. Each site costs $99 to $149 for an annual membership. That entitles you to unlimited email contacts with as many women as you can handle. Just be extra careful and bring lots of condoms.

If you're the kind of guy who lives to carve new notches into your headboard, your objective is to cast the widest net possible. And remember to include all of your favorite fetishes and activities in your profile. Since this is all about *your* pleasure, be blunt and straightforward in your descriptions. Say exactly what you want. And don't worry about political correctness.

Just remember that the swinging-sex site memberships are heavily weighted toward males. In fact, most of the sites we checked out had 10 or more males for every female. In many instances, there were more women looking for *women* than If there were looking for men. Even more alarming, there were sometimes more men looking for *men* than women looking for men.

Considering the sexually liberated people who join alternative lifestyle sites, perhaps the numbers are not so surprising. Gay men and women have fewer choices than straight people do. So it stands to reason they would gravitate toward the more open-minded online dating venues.

HOT TIP NUMBER 3 – *DO cast the widest net possible if you're the kind of guy who lives to carve new notches into your headboard. In other words, the fewer restrictions you put on the types of women you are willing to meet, the more women you will meet!*

If, on the other hand, you're ready to commit and share your life with someone, you can find "Ms. Right" on any number of more traditional dating sites. The key to finding her is detailing her as precisely as possible in your profile. If you have doubts or need a sounding board, talk to a good friend about it.

Sometimes friends can give you insights into your own personality that will help you refine your search. If writing clearly isn't your strong suit, find a friend who can write your profile for you based on your verbal description. It can make a huge difference in the quality of your responses.

If marriage is your goal, you can also try some of the mail-order bride sites. CherryBlossoms.com and RussianLadies.com are two of the better ones. CherryBlossoms.com claims it has arranged over 30,000 marriages since starting in 1974. Here you'll find thousands of attractive, marriage-minded women of all ages from all over Asia, South America and Europe.

If you are one of the many males who has developed a "thing" for Asian, Latin, European or Russian women, you might like this option.

No matter which site you search, the objective is to screen out those who don't fit your criteria and screen in those who do. Trust us when we say this is not as easy as it sounds. Your goal, when searching for Ms. Right, is to cast a narrow net. After all, you're only looking for "The One."

Remember that a picture and some words on your computer screen do not make a match any more than they make a marriage. To find the right marriage partner, you will need to make an investment. Life partners don't come easy. And they certainly should not be left to chance.

Meet as many women as you can face-to-face and sharpen your profile as often as it takes after each meeting to narrow the field. Ultimately, it's all going to come down to chemistry. Chemistry can be emotional, intellectual, spiritual or physical or all of them. Generally speaking, having one kind of chemistry isn't enough for the long haul. A long-term relationship needs more. Either you connect on multiple levels with a partner or you don't.

Once you have found the right kind of chemistry, it comes down to endurance. Does your relationship "have legs"? Will it last until you are old and toothless? Only time will tell. But choosing the right partner in the beginning could pay off big-time in the end. According to most studies, happily married men still live longer and healthier lives than single men.

So which do you really want? Ms. Right or Ms. Right Now? Do you covet a series of one-night stands, a live-in lover or marriage? Or maybe you just want someone to bungee jump with on weekends. With Internet dating, you can have all of the above or any combination.

Are You GU?

Welcome to the geography section. This is where you figure out just how far you are willing to travel to find your woman or women.

"GU" is dating parlance for "geographically undesirable." What makes a woman GU to you may not equal what makes her GU to your best buddy. Or what makes you GU to her. After all, everyone has limits. Your mileage may vary.

Think about it. Someone far away may suit guys with irregular dating patterns but turn a regular dating relationship into a chore. Someone right in your backyard may be convenient, but she may also be in your face more often than you want.

On most Internet dating sites, you can tailor your searches to those women within a 10-, 25 , 50- or 100-mile radius. You can search locally, regionally, nationally or internationally. It's entirely up to you. Let your budget, your time and your current gasoline prices guide you.

If money is no object, you can search across the country or the world. There are thousands of hot women, for example, in Little Rock, Arkansas and Fayetteville, North Carolina. Many would kill for a plane ticket to sunny Southern California, where we have the good fortune to reside. There are thousands more women in such exotic faraway places as Thailand, Romania, Singapore, Costa Rica and Sweden who would love to come to America and will work hard to "catch" an American male. We know many American men who have done well at this and found their beautiful mail-order brides. So why not you?

If you happen to be taking a business trip across the country or across one of the oceans, you can always set something up at your destination. If you visit certain places regularly, you might want a partner for fun and games while you're there. Pretend you're a sailor with a girl in every port, just for the heck of it.

If you hope to find love or lust in your backyard, set your first search to within a five- or 10-mile radius of your home. More if you live in a rural area where running to the grocery store is a 50-mile jaunt. Less if you live in a densely populated city such as New York. If you want a larger pool of women from which to choose, set your search for 100 miles or more. But if you happen to find your soul mate 100 miles away or 10,000 miles away, you may want to see her more often than geography, your budget or your busy schedules allow.

That's not to say that longer-distance relationships won't work. They can, and they do. But they only work for certain types of people. Are you that type?

We noticed that women tend to search longer distances than men. Many women are perfectly willing to travel 50 or 100 miles or more to find their match. We guys tend to want our women located closer to home. Could this be a sign of the changing times? After all, many of our fathers and most of our grandfathers wanted their women in the home. Today, we're lucky to merely have them close.

HOT TIP NUMBER 4 – *DO set your search to within a five- or 10-mile radius of your home if you want to find someone close. If you live in a rural area where running to the grocery store is a 50-mile jaunt, set 100 miles or more. If you live in a densely populated city such as New York, a five-mile radius will more than cover it.*

It's a Numbers Game

No matter who or what you want from Internet dating, success is a game of numbers. The more women you meet, the more likely you are to find exactly the kind of woman you want.

The hard part, if you meet lots of women, will be keeping them straight in your head. Remember their names and which details about yourself you have revealed to them. In addition to being a great test of memory, it will prevent you from repeating yourself or having your date think you suffer from Alzheimer's disease.

More hits on your profile usually lead to more emails. Include a photo in your profile and get eight times more hits, according to Match.com. More emails lead to more phone conversations. More phone conversations lead to more face meetings. And more face meetings increase the odds of "matching" someone right for you.

You should also know that most women online receive far more responses than most men do. We met one really plain woman who got over 3,500 hits and 150 emails in six weeks. Another woman told us she had received over 16,000 hits in less than 90 days. Still another woman we know, a 39-year-old knockout, received almost 140 emails in two weeks. Of those 140, she responded to four! Of course, she didn't have time to answer them all. She barely had time to read them all. And she was more shocked than we were by her sudden deluge of male suitors.

As we said earlier, Internet dating is a numbers game. And with most of the Internet dating sites, males simply outnumber females. Instead of the optimal 50-50 ratio of men to women, the real ratio on traditional Internet dating sites is probably closer to a male-dominated 70-30. So, marketing yourself successfully to these women means finding ways to differentiate yourself from other males. You are, after all, competing for a smaller pool of women.

Face reality. The more attractive the woman, the more hits and emails she will receive. And the harder it will be for you to get her attention, no matter how good-looking, rich or intelligent you are. She might not even want a physically attractive man. Women tend to place less value on looks than men. And she might be taking the aggressive approach to Internet dating. Women in this category are less inclined to respond to your email pitches. They would rather play huntress than hunted. In other words, she wants to choose rather than be chosen.

In pure marketing terms, the women of Internet dating are faced with an overwhelming number of buying decisions. It's the law of supply and demand. And true to their apparent genetic predisposition to shopping, women often like to sample before they buy. Get used to the fact that you will be sampled. And discarded for no apparent reason. But put yourself in their shoes: They have so many buying options they don't have time to explain each one in terms most males will understand.

As a friend once told us, Internet dating is like taking your sister shopping for shoes. If you take her to the Giant Shoe Emporium, she'll spend all day looking and never buy shoes. But if you take her to the Little Shoe Boutique, she'll have fewer buying decisions and probably make a purchase.

The same marketing-based theory holds true whether you live in a major metropolitan area or a town that just installed its first traffic light. There may not be as many beauties in a one-light town, but the ones who are there have far fewer buying decisions and will often make a purchase. You can fish in the ocean, or you can fish in a barrel. We don't have to tell you where you'll catch the most fish, do we?

To cut through the clutter, you'll have to get creative. Don't send that great-looking babe in the string bikini or sheer nightgown an email that says, "Hi" in the subject line. She gets hundreds of emails like that every day. Try a different approach and she just might hear you above the roar. Women like compliments. Start off with something like, "Love your tan." Keep in mind that there are lots of other guys thinking the same thoughts and holding onto the same hopes as you. Stand tall. Be different. Be responsive. Be flexible. And above all, be the ultimate man you are.

Since it's a numbers game, you'll want to keep a close watch on your time and bank account numbers. Put a time limit on your first meetings. Whether it's 15 minutes for you Type A personalities or an hour or more for you Type Bs, respect your time and hers. Then keep a healthy respect for your budget by setting a one-drink maximum. We call it the ODM.

The first meeting is absolutely not the time to spring for dinner, a show, a nightclub or a concert. The sheer numbers of women you'll meet could send you quickly to the poorhouse. Caveat emptor: If you don't have deep pockets, proceed with extreme caution and stay away from shallow women.

The Internet dating scene is just as much a numbers game for a woman as it is for you. We had several women email us when we first signed up. Apparently, they forgot they had done so. Because a month or so later, the same women emailed us again, as if for the first time. We got the feeling they were sending bunches of emails at a time, and weren't tracking their efforts very well. We were unimpressed by their disorganized, scattershot approach.

Look for clues in their profiles. Shallow, materialistic females often reveal themselves in their narratives about what they like and what they are looking for in men. Pay attention. Don't let her good looks override your ability to reason. After all, it is a numbers game. You can always find an attractive woman who is neither materialistic nor shallow. Just be patient, and you're likely to find exactly what you want on the Internet.

 **HOT TIP NUMBER 5** – *DO put a time limit on your first face-to-face meeting. Whether it's 15 minutes for you Type A personalities or an hour for you Type Bs, respect your time and hers. Keep a healthy respect for your budget, too, with a one-drink maximum, or ODM.*

Now that you know what you want, where to look and what to look for, it's time to zero in on the right online dating site. You can try more than one if you have the time and the energy, but it's usually smart to begin with one well-chosen site.

PART TWO:

The Art of Getting Noticed.

"Men who do not make advances to women are apt to become victims to the women who make advances to them."

– Walter Bagehot, 1826-1877

Setting Up Camp

Once you've figured out exactly what you're looking for, you need to find the right dating site for you. The best way to accomplish this is by "lurking" on various sites to see what each has to offer.

What is lurking? Lurking is when you can look at women's profiles but you cannot initiate contact. Women can contact you if your profile is online, but you cannot respond. Some sites won't even let you open the emails women write to you. Instead, they use them to tease you into signing up for a paid membership. Most dating sites will let you set up a profile and keep it active without cost. In other words, it's free.

Lurkers can window-shop all day long on most sites. They just can't buy anything until they've paid the cover price.

So what do you look for? You look for sites that seem to have the largest numbers of the types of women you'd like to meet. If you set your priorities correctly in the first chapter, you'll have an easier time with this chapter. Knowing what you want is half the battle. And since Internet dating is a numbers game, you will probably do well by starting on one or more of the larger, better-known dating sites.

At this writing, Match.com is the 400-pound gorilla of traditional Internet dating sites. Match.com began online dating in April 1995 and attracted over 60,000 singles. It quickly became a leading online matchmaking site. By early 1996, nearly 500,000 members were meeting on Match. Engagement and marriage announcements began pouring in. At this writing, there have been more than 1,300 marriages and at least 50 babies made by members. There are over 8 million members on Match, according to their recent TV commercials. Surely you can find a few hundred strong candidates there – enough to keep you busy for quite some time.

In addition to Match.com, there are also over 5 million members on yahoopersonals.com. Both Yahoo and Match allow lurking guys to read the emails women send. But other sites such as Udate.com and sister site Kiss.com do not.

The 800-pound gorilla of adult-oriented sites is AdultFriendFinder.com, with over 5 million members and 15 million more members on its global sister sites. Finding sex partners here, however, can be challenging. Males outnumber females by a wide margin.

During our searches, we checked out females from dozens of foreign countries. We "visited" several countries where thousands of men are looking for women, but only a few hundred women are looking for men. In the end, it's all about numbers. You can join one site or several if you want to increase your odds.

As long as you're setting up camp, you should also set up a free email account with *Yahoo!, hotmail* or one of the other free email hosts. It's probably not wise to use your real name in this email address. The idea is to have some fun while you maintain security and anonymity with an email address you can safely give out to the females you make contact with.

We had nine email accounts between us at one point. But only two contained our real names. Our strategy was simple.

Giving a female your "private" email address is like culling her from the herd. You differentiate yourself from other online suitors by singling out a female, then taking her offline (away from the dating service) into your own little cyber-world.

Profiles in Courage

Your Internet dating profile is your calling card. How do you create an attention-getting profile? The mechanics are pretty easy. Depending on which site you join, you'll be asked a series of click-on-the-button questions and two or more essay questions. You'll be prompted each step of the way.

You'll also be prompted to upload your photo(s). More on that a bit later.

First, let's focus on your profile; it's your online dating calling card. If you write well, then have at it. Feel free to be as creative as you want to be. But if writing is a real challenge for you, find someone who can help you express yourself clearly, succinctly and eloquently. If you can't find help, go to theultimatemansguide.com and email us. For a nominal fee, we'll help you craft a great profile.

Your objective is to provide a memorable glimpse of yourself. Think of it as fishing. Without good bait on your hook, the fish won't bite. It's the same with Internet dating. If you don't reveal yourself in your profile, women may think you're hiding something and quickly move on. And don't just give them a laundry list of all the activities you enjoy. Add color to it. Give it some nuance. Say something provocative. Not overtly sexual, but rather, thought-provoking or clever. Most of the women we met valued intelligence. And most were turned off by any kind of premature sexual overture.

Pick an interesting "handle" for yourself. That's the name you will go by while you're online. It can be your real name or a made-up name, as long as it's easy to remember for you and your female target audience.

Read the profiles other men put up. Study their essays. Do they sound hokey and false to you? How do you think they sound to women? Learn from them. Then use what you've learned to create a better profile for yourself. One woman we met online claimed to have studied a few hundred other women's profiles before she wrote her own. She said she wanted to differentiate herself. She studied and assessed her competition, then created a profile that set her apart from the crowd.

Here is an actual profile essay written by a 49-year-old Southern California man. We left it exactly as it was written. See how much you can learn from it:

> "I AM LOOK FOR A PERSON WHO LIKES TO HAVE FUN AND LIKES TO DO THINGS TOGEATHER. SHE HAS TO BE KINDA GOOD LOOKING WHO IS SWEET INSIDE AND DOESN'T HAVE A BIG MOUTH. A PERSON WHO LIKES TO COOK AND WORKS AND BEEN AT THIER JOB FOR A WHILE AND HAS A NICE VOICE AND DOESN'T YELL ALL THE TIME WHEN THEY OPEN THIER MOUTH. AND I AM A BREAST MAN."

The author would have been smart to have someone with writing skills help write his profile. A better picture would have helped, too. This guy looked as if he'd been hit on the head by one too many surfboards. At least he spelled "breast" correctly. And there was honesty in his writing.

Most dating sites also let you choose an opening line. This headline is your first opportunity to screen in the kinds of women you're after. If you're looking for your soul mate, say so. If you just want someone to hang out with, say so. If you can say it cleverly, that's even better.

Describe the kind of woman you're looking for in as much detail as possible. Not physical details unless they are the most important things to you. Describe her personality or philosophy of life or core values that mesh with yours. And, for God's sake, don't lie about your personal physical details. After all, you're gonna meet some of these women in the flesh. Nothing will bother her more than realizing you are nothing at all like your profile, you look nothing at all like your picture, and she's been reeled in by your little "bait and switch" tactic.

HOT TIP NUMBER 6 – *DO read the profiles other men put up. Study their essays. Do they sound hokey and false to you? How do you think they sound to women? Learn from them. Then use what you've learned to create a better profile for yourself.*

If you're 5'9", don't claim to be 6'4". Women hate being lied to about anything. As we learned through experience, many males and females lie about smoking habits and age. And if you lie about something seemingly minor, it's often assumed that you will lie about anything and everything. When the truth is revealed (as it usually is), you'll look like a liar, a fool or someone she'll tell others to avoid.

On the other hand, there are still a few women around who have big hearts full of forgiveness. Just ask Evan Marriott, the $19,000-a-year construction worker who became television's *Joe Millionaire*. When Evan chose Zora, he revealed one of the biggest lies of all time. He was not worth $50 million, or even $50 thousand. Zora, who was unimpressed by the $50 million to begin with, chose to overlook the lie and accepted Evan's ring. She and Evan also accepted the surprise million-dollar check from the show's producers. It was their reward for proving that love could win out over money. Their TV love, however, was short-lived. Not long after the show's season finale, the media reported that Evan and Zora had parted company, each with half a million in cash. And over 40 million viewers had already tuned in to witness their rather blissful TV reunion.

Don't claim to be "athletic" if you're clinically obese and haven't seen your feet in 10 years. Pressing buttons on a remote control does not constitute regular exercise. Repeatedly hoisting 12-ounce bottles of beer is not weight lifting. When a female suitor asks if you have a "six-pack," don't tell her it's in "the fridge."

Many women claim they are "into" things they may have only tried once. Like bungee jumping. She may have done it on a dare during her wild Mexican vacation but would never do it again on her own if her life depended on it. You just can't believe all the claims women or men make about the things they enjoy.

If she claims an interest you share, ask her a few probing questions about the activity to see if she has a genuine interest or she's merely posturing to impress you with her energy or athletic ability. If she claims to love football, ask her which team Jerry Rice plays for. Or who won last year's Super Bowl.

A woman's dating profile is like *Cliff's Notes*. It provides a brief summary but doesn't tell near the whole story. If you want the whole story, plan to spend the rest of your life with a woman. Even then, chances are pretty good that you still won't know all there is to know about her.

HOT TIP NUMBER 7 – *DON'T claim to be "athletic" if you're clinically obese and haven't seen your feet in 10 years. Pressing buttons on a remote control does not constitute regular exercise. Repeatedly hoisting 12-ounce bottles of beer is not weight lifting.*

Keeping It Fresh

You'll get more hits if you update your profile frequently. Each update moves your profile ahead in the line-up, where it will be seen by more women. We noted a marked increase in hits and emails immediately after each update. So we got into the habit of doing one or two updates each week. Without updates, our hit counts dropped to under 10 per day. With updates, we averaged 50 to 60 hits and at least 5 to 10 emails a day.

Be careful about what you change. If you add a new picture or type a new essay into your profile, you may disable your profile for up to 72 hours while the site censors do their thing. Of course, by using Alt.com or AdultFriendFinder.com, you won't have to contend with censorship at all.

On the other hand, a great new picture or a perfectly written essay on a more traditional dating site could increase your hit rate substantially. If you're smart, you'll sacrifice a couple of days worth of paltry hits for a few enhancements that could easily increase your hits by a couple of hundred percent.

Changing your answers to the multiple-choice questions will not disable your profile in any way. So it's okay to go a little crazy here. Just don't stray too far from the truth or you won't be happy with your responses. Don't claim to be a nonsmoker if you smoke like a chimney. Don't claim to drink socially if your refrigerator looks like a Coors commercial, you own a wet bar and your monthly liquor bill is higher than your car payment.

One of us tested out the profile update theory by revamping the other one's written profile and uploading a new picture. As soon as it appeared on the site, we got several dozen hits and a handful of emails from interested women, something we hadn't had in weeks.

In the end, how many hits you get is less important than the number of women who contact you via email. If you find yourself getting lots of hits and no emails, your profile probably needs a tune-up. It's not delivering the goods for you. The women are window-shopping but not buying.

Keep going back to the drawing board until you get it right. If you find the right woman or women, the extra trouble will be worth it.

HOT TIP NUMBER 8 – *DO update your profile frequently. Each update moves your profile ahead in the line-up to be noticed by more women.*

Win With Words of Wit and Wisdom

We'll admit that men with well-written profiles have an unfair advantage, at least in the beginning. Whether writing a profile or an email (or a book about Internet dating), some men know how to turn a phrase for maximum impact. And there are lots of women who appreciate a man who expresses himself clearly. So if you're having trouble making your point, or getting to the point, enlist help from a friend who can write well.

In a medium virtually ruled by email, being a skilled, persuasive writer can be to your advantage. Of course, this advantage only helps at the beginning of the process, when writing is the sole form of communication. Once you meet someone face-to-face, you are pretty much on a level playing field with every other guy, unless you can also communicate well verbally.

And remember Ryan, who wooed and won the lovely Trista on TV's *The Bachelorette?* Ryan, a Colorado firefighter, separated himself from the pack of 25 eligible males early on by writing beautiful poetry inspired by Trista herself. In the end, his special "way with words" inspired Trista to choose Ryan over everyone else and accept his marriage proposal.

The show was so popular, it won the weekly ratings war by a landslide. The ability to write well and romance appear to be ratings winners.

HOT TIP NUMBER 9 – *DO ask a friend with persuasive writing skills to help with your profile if you have trouble writing. It will make a big difference in the number of hits and emails you receive.*

PART THREE:

The Ultimate Rules of Engagement.

"You don't know a woman until you have had a letter from her."
– Ada Leverson, 1865-1936

Clicking by Clicking

At this point, you should know what you want and which Internet dating site you'll be searching from. You can search aggressively (send lots of emails), passively (wait for emails to come to you) or combine aggressive and passive tactics. More on this later.

If you decide to be aggressive, you'll be the one checking hundreds of profiles and sending out "feeler" emails. An interesting subject line and a quick written message accompanied by your profile will usually do the trick.

As we said earlier, you can use the customized search criteria you developed in Chapter 1, including:

age
astrological sign
height
body type
hair
eye color
profession
income
education
ethnic background
religious preferences
marital status
smoking/drinking
whether or not you want kids

You should also look at a woman's online activity. Match.com and other sites, for example, tell you how long it's been since a woman was last online. If her profile says she was last seen two weeks ago or longer, she might have found someone else already. Your odds of getting a response from her are slim to none. But if she's been online during the last 24 to 48 hours, she's still actively looking. Keep that in mind when you start firing off emails to female prospects.

If you begin corresponding with a woman but see that she is still actively searching online, you can pretty much write off any chance you may have had with her. Her online activity reveals that she is still looking for someone other than you. On the other hand, if you see that she's been inactive for several days or weeks, she is likely interested enough in you to have suspended her search.

Check your spelling and learn the "language" of email. Learn what emoticons (those little smiley faces) are and what they mean. Learn that BTW means "by the way." Learn the difference between LOL (laughing out loud) and ROFL (rolling on the floor laughing), and learn that "k" means okay. And if you write in all capital letters, people will think you're screaming at them. In the world of online dating, email is one of your primary tools. Learn to use it wisely and well.

Don't expect women to respond too quickly to your emails. In fact, don't necessarily expect them to respond at all. Just know that some will respond some of the time. If the women are extremely attractive, expect to wait several days for a response. Remember these women may be getting hammered by hundreds of hits and dozens of emails every day. Attractive women, who may get up to 1,000 hits or more a week, may respond to you in one to three days or more. Beyond a week or so, you can safely assume she's overwhelmed by emails or not interested, especially if you see her online.

If you decide to be passive, you will basically sit back and wait to see who comes to you. Just realize that, by taking a passive approach, you are leaving a great deal more to chance and you are less likely to hit your bulls-eye in a short period of time. On the positive side, the women who email you will already be predisposed toward you.

You can also combine aggressive and passive tactics. You can be selectively aggressive or selectively passive. Let some women come to you while you seek out and contact those who catch your eye. Over time, you will find the strategy that works best for you.

On Match.com, you'll also find compatibility ratings. These are based on your answers to the multiple-choice profile questions. Your customized "match list" will show you women who match with you in descending order from 100% to about 90%. From our experience, these ratings are virtually meaningless.

Matching on paper and matching in person are two entirely different concepts. We met many women we had much in common with, but that was all we had. It's not enough to have several things in common with a woman. On the TV show *Married by America*, a panel of noted psychologists hired to eliminate one of the newly engaged couples said their couple was a perfect match on paper. But there was zero chemistry between the pair. We'd be willing to bet they were astrologically mismatched, too.

To find out if you really click with someone, you'll need time and an eventual face-to-face meeting. Use your dating site's email service to deliver your profile to your target honey. Compose your email and attach your profile to it. Don't repeat what you said in your profile. Be clever. Be witty. Be funny. Be sensitive. Be impulsive. Be enlightened. And above all, be different.

Some women believe in fate and might email you based on some computer's compatibility calculation. Why not? After all, most women who come to you first are already interested.

If it's true that a woman can decide within five minutes whether she will sleep with you, having her *find you* is 75% of the game. This is a good stratagem for guys who just want to score.

You'll also need to know something about Eastern and Western astrological compatibility. Our experience has taught us that astrology is a pretty good predictor of compatibility. That's why we've included individualized astrological profiles and compatibility ratings for each sign of the zodiac and all its potential partners later in this book.

As bogus as some of you may think astrology is, you should take it very seriously, for it holds many basic truths. One of us is an Aquarian who limited most of his searches to Aquarius, Gemini and Sagittarius women, knowing he tended to "click" best with these signs.

And, like it or not, you've only got a nanosecond and 10 words or less to click with someone via email, so make the most of it. Find something in her profile you can relate to. For example, if she says she loves gourmet cooking, your subject line might say something like, "Here's a recipe for…" or "Medium rare…" It has a much better chance than "Hi."

Just look for clues in her profile. Women love knowing they're being listened to and heard. Show her you're paying attention. And be patient. It may take her up to several days to get back to you. But if you've done your homework, you'll hear from her. You may even end up with her home phone number.

HOT TIP NUMBER 10 – *DO look for something you can relate to in a woman's profile. Then address your email to that topic. It will help you cut through the email clutter on her computer.*

Hide and Seek for Adults

There will be times when you feel as though you're playing the adult version of "Hide and Go Seek." At its most extreme, this means hiding your profile. In fact, that is probably the ultimate secret weapon for the aggressive Internet dater.

On Match.com, and many other sites, you can literally hide your profile so it does not appear online. This frees you to create your very own foxhunt without interference. You can see the foxes, but they cannot see you until you pounce.

In love and war, the element of surprise nearly always favors the predator. Just make sure you attach the right profile and photo, the right subject line and the right email message. If you make just the right approach, it's game, set and Match.com.

In our experience, more women than men use this tactic. When she's drop-dead gorgeous and taking over 1,000 hits a day, it's hard to play predator. She barely has time to download and scan her incoming emails for an interesting subject line. There are just too many buying decisions. That's why these women prefer to shop from their own neatly written grocery lists.

The more passive-aggressive types can hide their profiles for days or weeks at a time in order to buy more time to process incoming emails and profiles. This is also a good time to hone your profile into the polished little gem it will have to be if you want to stay competitive. You can easily manipulate the system to suit your changing moods or your changing mind.

If your nature is passive, just keep your profile open and available to every female in cyberspace. It's the ultimate secret weapon for those who hate tempting fate. If you are purely passive, you will find adventure and discovery in this process, even though you will be limiting your responses to a pool of women who are attracted to you instead of women you are attracted to. You may enjoy the fact that these women have already made 75% of their buying decision.

Of course, after a few months of this, you may begin to think Chinese water torture sounds like fun. You may suddenly find yourself pulling your profile offline and going predatory. Maybe you're tired of sitting back and accepting what comes to you. Maybe you're just plain tired.

We played the hide-and-seek game several times. We hid our profile for several days or a week at a time in order to catch our breath and play predators. Then, within a day of revealing our profiles once again, we found several new female emails waiting in our inboxes.

HOT TIP NUMBER 11 – *DO hide your profile from time to time so it does not appear online. This frees you to create a foxhunt without interference. You can see the foxes, but they cannot see you until you pounce. In love and war, the element of surprise nearly always favors the predator.*

PART FOUR:

Enhance Your Image. Decode Hers.

"What attracts us in a woman rarely binds us to her."

– John Churton Collins, 1848-1908

Are You Looking at Me?

When it's time to upload your picture, make sure you have a good one. It should be recent enough to look like you do today. One of us met a woman who claimed to be 43 years old. Her profile picture was softly focused, but she looked fairly attractive and several years younger than her claimed age. When we met, I knew she had to be 58, with badly thinning hair, a bald spot and wrinkles that made the Grand Canyon look like flat land. Her online photo was not even in the ballpark of recent. It had to be 15 years old!

Your picture should also show some character. It should help you put your best foot forward. One of us uploaded a head and shoulders tuxedo shot that got over 2,200 hits and over 190 emails from interested women in an eight-week stretch. The intensely mischievous half-grin and the elegant black tuxedo must have created or fed a certain kind of fantasy in some women's minds.

If you count the number of women who claim the ability to go from "blue jeans to blueblood formal affairs in no time flat," you'll gain some key clues about what they're looking for or fantasizing about. Needless to say, the tux turned out to be the perfect bait for attracting certain kinds of women. Many were upscale, uptown Mercedes/BMW/Lexus/Jaguar-driving women. They were successful in real estate, marketing, investing and other entrepreneurial ventures. In many cases, they earned six-figure-incomes.

One woman told us the tuxedo almost stopped her from sending a first email. She admitted she was a jeans and T-shirts kind of person and the tuxedo almost turned her off. Almost.

So we're not suggesting that every guy run out and get a tuxedo for his photo shoot or even that a tux is the best thing to wear for your shoot. We are suggesting that you do something a little different with your picture. If you like animals, add your favorite pet to the shot. If you really like participating in sports, have someone take an action shot. If you're a comedian, do something funny. Whether you add a pet, a prop or a favorite hangout to your shot, strive to be the ultimate man you can be.

We even tried putting our baby pictures up to see how many hits we'd get. After all, women are generally maternal. We thought the baby pictures would a) appeal to their maternal instincts and b) reveal our more sensitive sides. The baby pictures, by the way, worked well. Just remember that your picture may or may not appeal to a certain type of woman. Ask yourself if that's the kind of woman you really want to reach, and present yourself accordingly.

Differentiation is one of the keys to successful marketing. Being able to prove you're different is another key. In other words, you need to be able to show how you're different from all the other men who are out there trying.

Her picture also says something about her. While the majority of women on sites such as Match.com post very tasteful photos, we found a few who took a more seductive approach. There were occasional bikini shots or lingerie shots that revealed lots of leg or cleavage. We estimate that some of these women attract 1,000 hits a day or more. We also estimate that the smiling fat lady wearing the funny hat and swinging a golf club gets very few hits.

And don't assume that any woman is sexually available just because she posts a "sexy" picture. Every man has his own idea about what constitutes a sexy picture. So does every woman. Remember that women will make assumptions about you from your photo, too. When we posted our tuxedo shot, we received dozens of emails from women who either fantasized about James Bond or were only interested in a companion for black tie events and fundraisers.

In Internet dating, as in life, you're better off not assuming anything about anyone. In some cases, you can't even assume the picture posted is the person in the profile. One woman uploaded a picture of actress Catherine Zeta-Jones on her profile. We were appalled by her obvious deceit.

Remember, don't use an old picture of yourself. Since you are likely to meet some of the women who see your profile, get a good current shot or a shot that looks pretty much the way you look now. It can even be a year old or two, but it has to look as you look now.

HOT TIP NUMBER 12 – *DO post a recent picture – one that looks as you look today. Many women complained to us that the men they were meeting didn't look anything like the pictures they posted online.*

What You See Is Not Always What You Get

Each one of us has the mental capacity to make the beautiful uglier and the ugly more beautiful. Beauty truly is in the eye of the beholder.

That same girl you once rejected because her feet were too large or her lipstick was too dark might just be the perfect girl for you today. She might have a heart of gold and not an evil, man-hating or angry bone in her body.

Maybe she's the sweetest, kindest, warmest-hearted person you've ever met. Maybe she'll do anything to make you happy. Maybe she'll love you unconditionally. In the end, if you give her half a chance, it might be her *inner beauty* that overrides your perception of her outer beauty or reality.

She just might be the perfect woman for you today and always.

One thing is certain: If you look for flaws, you will find them. If you look for virtues, you will find them, too. What you think you see is not always what you get.

Playing the Internet Dating Game

If you're one of those boys with lots of toys, keep it to yourself until you've dated someone for a while. The "stuff" you think will impress women you meet for the first time won't. Many women told us that, in addition to men lying about physical qualities, their second-greatest turnoff is men bragging about their possessions early on. One woman claimed she was propositioned with material possessions on the *first date*. The proposition went something like this: "You know, I have a very secluded beach home in Mexico. The only thing missing is you. So why don't I fly you down there next weekend and we'll have some fun with my new jet skis."

This woman was definitely not impressed. She declined the offer.

Many women see this as a sure sign of insecurity in males. We brag about our stuff because we lack in more substantive areas like character, intelligence, humor, sincerity, humility, compassion or other core qualities. Droning on about your new "Beamer" or "Harley," your house in the Bahamas or your 60-foot sailing yacht won't necessarily get your date out of her clothes and into your arms.

Unless she's a gold-digger of the first magnitude, she probably doesn't care about your fancy toys. At least, not on the first date. So try hard not to default to bragging about your stuff. If you can't find something interesting to talk with her about, she's not for you, no matter how good-looking she is.

If you can't come up with a better way to impress a woman, and your only goal is to score, then sign up on Alt.com or AdultFriendFinder.com. There are plenty of women there who will share your toys in exchange for sex. Some of them value "generosity," so prepare to be generous. We suspect that some of them are professional "working girls." In the end, it's probably less expensive and more efficient to hire a hooker. How you pay for sex is up to you.

Sure, some women are impressed with wealth and power. Some will reveal that in their profiles. But many are not. Many women are searching for more enduring qualities in a date or a mate. According to *Men's Health* magazine, women value your genuine interest in having a relationship. They value intelligence, humor, financial security, wisdom, maturity, honesty and availability. To many women, great looks, expensive toys and a well-honed six-pack are secondary considerations.

Understand, too, that women are generally less visually oriented than we are when it comes to attraction. Accept the fact that your good looks may not be enough to get you past her filters. Accept the fact that the female brain is often capable of processing more information from more stimuli than yours. Get over it. Move on.

Pay attention to the desired age ranges preferred by the women you're checking out. If she's 40 and she wants a guy between 25 and 36, she's probably hankering for a slim hard-body who can surf on her waterbed with her. Of course, she might also be immature or living in the past. On the other hand, there are many 30-year-old babes who say they want someone 40 to 60 with a six-figure income. Can you say, "Sugar Daddy"? We knew you could.

HOT TIP NUMBER 13 – *DO pay attention to the desired age ranges preferred by the women you're checking out. If she's 40 and she wants a guy between 25 and 36, she's probably hankering for a slim hard-body who can surf on her waterbed with her.*

Most members also post their occupations and income levels on their profiles. More revealing than that, they post the desired income levels for their prospective mates. You'll find other clues to your mystery woman here. If she's looking for someone with a six-figure income, reread the end of the paragraph above.

If you see an appealing woman who is "new" to the site, approach her quickly and without hesitation while she is fresh. Move as fast as you can. If you procrastinate, others will jump ahead of you and, perhaps, win her favor.

If you want the game to work for you, *you've got to work at it*. Finding the right woman – the woman who will not only rock your world but make it a better place for you – will require a great deal of your time and intelligence.

If you want to play the game, learn to play it well.

The Women of Internet Dating

There are millions of women in the online dating pool. And they don't all fall into the stereotyped profiles we've created below. There are many women, just as there are many men, who simply defy stereotypes. In fact, the majority of women we met were nice, normal people with nice, normal lives. They don't fit any of the stereotypes below. There were also some women who not only fit the stereotypes, but actually defined them.

For every stereotype described below, there is a male counterpart. And there are negative stereotypes that apply only to men. One that comes immediately to mind is the "lounge lizard." He's the guy with the slick hair, the gold chains around his neck and the leisure suit trying to smooth-talk every woman at the bar.

Stereotypes can be good or bad. As you read the descriptions below, some may strike you as being attractive and some not so attractive.

By learning to spot the types of women described below, you'll save yourself a great deal of time and money, and possibly heartache, along the way.

The Shooting Star

This one has everything going for her but endurance. You find yourself liking everything about her. She's great-looking. She has a killer personality and a beautiful spirit. She's a poster child for "T and A." You'll connect with her on so many levels that you find yourself thinking she's "The One." Then, just as you are getting comfortable with the idea, usually after several promising dates, she suddenly evaporates into thin air and sucks all the wind from your sails.

The Future Ex-Wife

Has already been married once or twice and has not learned a thing about having a successful give-and-take relationship. Her nagging ways and annoying habits are hard-wired into her and cannot be changed no matter how well you treat her. She's destined to repeat her own history by turning you into yet another ex-husband with alimony, child support and no place to live.

The Self-Closer

Any female you meet who convinces herself that you are "The One." She'll save you the trouble by talking herself into bed with you, usually within three dates. She'll also call and/or email you often with all sorts of suggestive remarks. We can think of worse things than letting her seduce you, so go for it. Isn't that the reason why you're here? Proceed with caution.

The Gold-Digger

Her profile may contain such phrases as "accustomed to the finer things in life" or "love dressing up and traveling to Europe" or "attends frequent fundraisers." She might list her favorite TV show as *Lifestyles of the Rich & Famous*. She's likely to be "model" pretty and dressed to the nines in her profile photo. If you don't drive a BMW or Porsche and earn a high six-figure income, run as fast as you can in the other direction. She will ask what kind of car you drive or how your stock portfolio is doing before she asks your name.

The Drama Queen

To her, everything in life is a big deal. She's got more issues than *TIME* magazine and more crises than the Middle East. It's even worse if she *admits* she's a drama queen. This woman will make many demands on you. She's the epitome of high maintenance. She's a headache without aspirin. If you overlook those qualities and chase her for her stunning good looks or beautiful heart-shaped butt, you will suffer mightily. You're a glutton for punishment. Seek psychiatric help immediately.

The Predator
She'll eat you alive. She's the cannibal of online dating. She wants what she wants when she wants it. If you're smart, it won't be you that she wants. It will be some other guy whom you don't like. Avoid her like the plague, unless you're strong enough to handle a truly blistering one-night stand.

The Madonna
If platonic relationships with the opposite sex are your thing, this might be the girl for you. She doesn't drink or smoke or listen to hard rock. To her, holding hands is the same as getting to second base. She wants only to be pure of heart and mind and body; all at your cost. Just remember: Her chastity belt is a heavy burden to bear.

The Thrill-Seeker
Avoid her at all costs, unless you are a thrill-seeker, too. Otherwise, her penchant for jumping out of planes and rock-climbing will surely lead you to a premature heart attack. And unless you live on a farm with no neighbors in sight, avoid having her as an overnight guest. Her screaming and yodeling in the bedroom are sure to get the neighborhood dogs howling, and you won't get 10 minutes of sleep. On the plus side, she'll probably agree to nude bungee jumping on the first date. Unbridled enthusiasm on your part here will pretty much guarantee peak sexual encounters for everyone. Just remember: Whether you

nail her in the boardroom, the bedroom or a public restroom, she won't be happy unless you're going 200 miles an hour with your hair on fire.

The Single Mom
Face it. The kid(s) is (are) number one in this triangle. And that's how it will be for the foreseeable future, especially if the kid(s) is (are) still in diapers when you meet. No matter how good-looking or nice she is, she's a mommy first and everything else second. If you like kids, avoid meeting hers for as long as possible. A year is probably a good target to shoot for, if mom lets you hold out that long. Then meet the kid(s) if you and mom are still clicking. Just remember that it's harder to break up with two or more people than it is to break up with one. And, if it all works out, you'll get to be a stepdad.

The Soccer Mom
She's got two or three kids, a minivan and a big slobbering dog. They will be your constant companions for the duration of your relationship. Can you handle it?

The Empty-Nester
The kids have grown up and moved out, and mom suddenly finds herself free and in need of male companionship. She's older, but wiser and more experienced. Unlike many younger women, she also knows what she wants. You won't need to guess, because she'll tell you. We can think of worse dates for the ultimate man.

The Temptress
Dark, sultry and exploding with volcanic sexuality, this type of woman can turn you on with a smoldering glance. But unThe

ware: Like the black widow spider, her bite can be lethal. Proceed with caution.

The Golf Widow

Where did she get that stupid-looking hat? Does anyone really find *that* attractive? Frankly, we're glad we weren't around when she discovered her interest in golf. Hole in one, anyone? Only other old duffers need apply.

The Damsel in Distress

She's looking for someone to save her from something or someone. Better decide up front if you want her crises to become your crises. While it is sometimes gratifying to rescue a woman (everyone needs a little extra help at times), it is unhealthy to make a habit of it. Get involved with this one at your own peril, for her life may be filled with crises, and the cost of continually rescuing her may be way too high for your emotional and financial budget.

The Bitch

Some women are just never happy. This one will do everything in her power to lure you into her web of misery. She complains constantly. She dislikes you before she knows you. And she takes no personal responsibility for any of it. Everything that's wrong with her life is someone else's fault. She's a victim with a bad attitude. Date her only if you love misery. Better yet, consider seeking professional help.

The Rediscovered Slut

If you just want a sex partner, you could do a lot worse than this one. Now that her kids are grown and they've flown the coop, Mom wants to make up for lost time. She wants to experience all the sexual variations she missed out on during 15 years of marriage. She might spike her hair and wear tight mini-dresses. She loves talking about sex and thinking about sex. Enjoy!

The Dreamer

She writes poetry, spikes her purple hair and wears granny dresses. She talks about all the things she's going to accomplish "someday." That pretty much describes her sex life, too. Someday, you might get her out of her granny dress. Someday, you might discover what treasures or treachery lie beneath. Sure, patience is a virtue, but this is ridiculous.

The Perpetual Wife

Unless you're looking for a wife who does wifely things, stay away from this one. She wants another ring on her finger, a white picket fence and someone around to nag with perpetual honey-do lists. She is incapable of enjoying her own company, much less your company. Don't even go there unless you're a glutton for punishment.

The Ice Queen

She's cool, attractive and sarcastic to a fault. You'll know her by her icy response to your innocently probing first email. Either she doesn't answer you at all, or she shoots you, a near-total stranger, a one-line put-down that makes you scratch your head and say, "Huh?" Next!

The Good Christian Woman

Unless you are a good Christian man, you might want to pass on this one. She's a regular churchgoer looking for a storybook romance complete with once-a-year missionary sex under the covers in the dark. Chances are, she has lots of "rules" governing her life and behavior. If you cannot turn this into a religious experience, forget about it.

The "Program" Girl

Some women are like some men. This one doesn't want any commitments. She's just looking for a good time. She may even be looking to add a few notches to her bedpost. Which makes her a perfect match for the guy who just wants a regular female on his "program" (of regular sex partners). You fit her into your busy schedule when she can fit you into hers. Since sex is implicit in this "relationship," make sure you keep lots of condoms available. Because you'll also be sleeping with everyone she's ever slept with. Program Girls tend to sleep around just like Program Guys.

The Speed Queen

She's smart, busy and aggressive. She wants instant gratification. By the second or third email, she's giving you her cell phone number and asking for yours. She's pressing for a face-to-face meeting, however brief, to see if there's any "chemistry" with you. Best advice: If she has passed your email and photo requirements, go for it. If you pass her face-to-face meeting requirements, you may be doing the horizontal mambo with her by the second date.

The Biker Chick

She's a dyed-in-the-wool Harley-Davidson fan. She might be an owner or a rider. Either way, the throaty roar of 1000cc of chromed-out Harley power between her legs is sure to arouse her more primitive sensibilities. And she just might give you the ride of your life.

The Friend

Did you ever meet a really cool female you liked hanging out and doing things with, but you didn't want to have sex with? And who ever said your Internet dating search could only be for sex partners, romantic interests and wives? Why can't friendship be an option? Not sex. Not romance. Just good, old-fashioned friendship. She's the one who will join you in activities your romantic and sex partners won't. Just make sure she knows where you stand on the sex and romance issues for now. Be honest. And be open to the possibility that, somewhere down the road, she might become more than a friend. There are far worse places than friendship for romance to blossom.

The Right One

Only you will know it when you find her. One of us did. If you do, be sure and send your story to us for inclusion in our next book at: stories@theultimatemansguide.com.

PART FIVE:

Discover What You Really Want.

"*A relationship is what happens between two people who are waiting for something better to come along.*"
– Anonymous

The Rules of Internet Dating
(Hint: They're Your Rules)

The beauty of Internet dating is that there are no rules other than the ones you make up as you go. Think of the Internet as a really big candy store, and think of yourself as the proverbial kid. Any way you slice it, it's your movie and all the women are merely bit players until you find your co-star.

You can search in faraway countries or your own backyard. You can meet and date as many women as you desire or as few. If you have the time, money and energy, you can see four or five women every weekend, or you can see a couple each month.

You can set yourself up in a local coffee shop and have different women come to you every hour on the hour if you want. After a tough week at the office, we can think of worse ways to spend your Friday evening or your weekend.

When we started, we didn't have a clue about the process, the pitfalls or the probabilities. We learned as we went.

The first thing we learned was not to play big spender. It won't impress her, and it might bankrupt you. That's why we established the ODM, or one drink maximum, for all first meetings. If the female offered to pay for her own drink, we welcomed her independence. After all, we reasoned, she's making an investment, too. Though not all women who offer to pay are being sincere. The insincere ones will cave quickly when you insist on paying.

The bottom line on dating: Men still pay 75% of the time. And springing for dinner does *not automatically* entitle you to an evening of unbridled sexual heat.

You can make your own rules about responding to emails, too. Some guys will want to respond to every woman who sends them an email. After all, as we said earlier, she has already made

75% of her buying decision, so why not give her every consideration?

But if you value your time, you should be selective. Otherwise, you may end up with dozens of email pen pals, face-to-face meetings that go nowhere and very little free time left on your hands.

HOT TIP NUMBER 14 – *DO search in faraway countries or your own backyard. You can meet and date as many women as you desire or as few. If you have the time, money and energy, you can see four or five women every weekend, or a couple each month.*

The Hits Just Keep Coming... and Coming

We've talked a good deal about the numbers of hits people get on Internet dating sites. But hits don't tell the whole story. Having someone look at your profile counts as a hit, whether they make contact afterward or not. Hits are like window shopping.

So getting thousands of hits without contact is useless for you. You want those emails to come instead. As we said earlier, women who send you emails have already made 75% of their buying decision. If you're charming enough to get a face-to-face meeting, you're pretty much home free.

If five or 10 women out of every 100 who view your profile actually send you emails, your profile and picture are doing quite well for you. In fact, if you look at it in pure marketing terms, you're a raging success. Even the best direct-mail marketing programs see a 2% response rate as favorable.

If 20 women email you for every 1,000 hits your profile receives, you'll be quite busy sending emails, chatting on the phone and meeting for coffee or drinks. Most guys only have the time and energy to meet two or three women a week out of the 100 or more women who may appear on their "match" list.

Match lists are prepared by the online dating service to give members a starting point in their searches. By comparing answers given to the multiple-choice questions provided in each profile, the service compiles lists of members who match "on paper."

Hits are nice, but contacts (emails) are best. Look at it from your perspective. How many profiles and pictures do you look at? How many emails do you send? See what we mean?

We had match lists with over 200 women on them. Out of 200 women, only three or four were interesting enough or attractive enough at any one time to email. But a hit was registered each time we looked at a profile, anyway.

As one of our Internet dating friends said, "What good are a million hits if nobody sends you an email?" So if your buddy brags about the 5,000 hits he got, ask how many actually contacted him. Any fewer than 100 emails and he isn't doing very well, after all. He's getting less than the standard 2% response.

HOT TIP NUMBER 15 – *DO count your responses. If five or 10 women out of every 100 who view your profile actually send you emails, your profile and picture are doing quite well for you. If you look at it in pure marketing terms, you're a raging success.*

PART SIX:

Follow the Stars to Your Ultimate Co-Star.

*"That's the nature of women…
not to love when we love them,
and to love when we love them not."*
— Miguel de Cervantes, 1547-1616

Astrologically Speaking: Making Sure Your Stars Line Up

As you search your way through the Internet dating maze, nothing will be more helpful to you, in our opinion, besides knowing what you want, than astrology. As we've discovered in our own relationships, there's a great deal of truth in the astrological musings about compatibility, especially where romance is concerned.

The general rule of thumb is that your most compatible signs will be related signs. Fire signs (Aries, Leo and Sagittarius) generally go best with other fire signs. Water signs (Cancer, Scorpio and Pisces) go with other water signs. Ditto for earth signs (Taurus, Virgo and Capricorn) and air signs (Aquarius, Libra and Gemini). These groupings are the core of Western astrology.

And what about Eastern astrology – the Chinese calendar? Were you born in the year of the Tiger, the Ox, the Snake, the Dog or the Monkey? What personality traits go with each of those signs? Who are you most compatible with?

Whether you're looking for sex, companionship, love or marriage, the profiles that follow will help you craft a better approach for each of the 12 female sun signs and each of the 12 Chinese zodiac signs. You might notice that the language of these profiles is different than the rest of this book. That's because we copied them from other websites. You can find the unedited versions at newagedirectory.com, iVillage.com and SunnCity.com.

THE CAPRICORN WOMAN *(December 22–January 19):*

How to win her: She seeks status and security. If she likes you, she might hitch a ride with you and become your manager or cheerleader. Show her some potential for a future. She's a family-oriented traditionalist. She's also earthy with a smoldering sex drive. But she has to get to know you before she can love you. Be patient. After she comes around, she'll rather stay home with you than go out socially, unless socializing has something to do with your careers and finances.

How to lose her: She won't like it if you make disparaging remarks about her family. She won't give up her friends for you, either. Don't force her into your social agenda unless it involves business or finances. Avoid being critical about her personality or likes and dislikes. She prefers time to think and won't make snap judgments. Don't expect her to jump into your new, modern lifestyle. She's married to conventions.

Her best bets are: Taurus, Virgo, Scorpio, Pisces

Her worst bets are: Gemini, Leo, Libra, Aquarius, Aries

50-50: Cancer, Sagittarius, Capricorn

THE AQUARIUS WOMAN *(January 20–February 21):*

How to win her: She's smart and creative. She daydreams about the workings of the universe. She's a little "out there" and always comes up with weird ideas. Talk to her about her weird ideas. Accept that her friends come from every class of society and she likes them all regardless. She'll like you more if you like them, too. She's attracted to people who are intellectual, knowledgeable, artistic and interesting. She will be loyal to you if you are to her, so throw away the little black book. She needs freedom from convention and won't tolerate a restrictive environment. Cut her some slack. She expects you to be sincere, honest and open.

How to lose her: She can't stand arrogance or people who make demands. Don't criticize how she dresses or interacts with people, or you'll lose her respect. Don't ridicule her or laugh at her secret thoughts, or you'll never hear them again. Don't try to force your old-fashioned ideas or habits on her. She lives in the future and will likely rebel against accepted styles, rules and conventions.

Her best bets are: Gemini, Sagittarius, Aquarius, Libra

Her worst bets are: Aries, Capricorn, Taurus, Cancer, Virgo

50-50: Leo, Scorpio, Pisces

THE PISCES WOMAN *(February 22–March 21):*

How to win her: There is something mysterious and intriguing about this woman that you just can't figure out. Join the club. She'll purr like a kitten if you show her that you are a caring but dominant male with sufficient resources to provide for her needs. She is quite pliable, but be careful: She can break all too easily. With her, love is a guessing game. You're always guessing whether she loves you or not. Tell her your feelings about her. Compliment or reassure her from time to time. Keep everything, including your conversation, upbeat. She may have old-fashioned values, but she's just modern enough to believe in equal rights. She's quite traditional.

How to lose her: She needs to express her opinions. And she's going to do it whether you like it or not. Stifling her is a good way to end it. If you carry on about negative things, she'll fall into depression. She's looking to you for leadership, so don't waffle on her or fail to make a decision. It could be a deal-breaker.

Her best bets are: Cancer, Scorpio, Taurus, Gemini, Virgo, Capricorn

Her worst bets are: Aries, Leo, Sagittarius, Libra

50-50: Aquarius, Pisces

THE ARIES WOMAN *(March 22–April 20)*.

How to win her: You can influence her by being well read, knowledgeable and cultured. Don't try to force your opinions or wishes upon her. She rails at being bossed around. That's because she wants to be the boss. Instead, appeal to her logic and reason and sympathy to get your point across. She may be aggressive when you meet, and she'll always let you know where you stand with her. She likes to smother her man with motherly attention, so let her. She is sympathetic to others' needs, so she'll listen to yours. She likes being around people, so introduce her to your friends. She likes to be a social butterfly, but she will remain loyal to you. She likes to get out and lead, so give her space and let her burn off some energy. She often makes decisions without thinking of the consequences, so be prepared to bail her out.

How to lose her: Don't criticize her in front of others or suggest that she is wrong. She'll become very unpleasant and combative. Don't boss her around or give her orders. She'll develop a fanatical obsession that she is right. Don't appeal to her with reason and suggestions that appear to be constructive ideas or options. Get overly friendly with her female friends, and she'll go ballistic on you. She gets jealous easily. Don't be inattentive about your own appearance. She hates slovenliness.

Her best bets are: Leo, Sagittarius, Taurus, Aquarius

Her worst bets are: Gemini, Scorpio, Cancer, Pisces

50-50: Aries, Virgo, Libra, Capricorn

THE TAURUS WOMAN *(April 21–May 20):*

How to win her: Flattery gets you everywhere with this affectionate sentimentalist. Even if she feels you are putting one over on her, she can't resist compliments. Give her gifts with sentimental meaning. They don't have to be expensive (although it helps). Your gifts should celebrate things such as your first date, etc. She loves affection and old-fashioned chivalry. Give her a card with a poem that you wrote (or you found in a book). She's a hopeless romantic and appreciates things that are steeped in tradition. You could serenade her beneath her window, but you'll need a good voice. She loves a good conversation and she can engage you on a wide variety of subjects. Be reserved, but not aloof. She likes mystery and intelligence. She likes being wined and dined. She likely takes pride in her cooking skills, so compliment her cooking and she'll stuff you like a Thanksgiving turkey.

How to lose her: Don't be a cheapskate. Her nature is to be generous. She likes harmony and tranquility, so don't try to engage her in an argument or a harsh discussion. If you see she has an opinion about something, don't try to change it. Don't try to force her into something against her will.

Her best bets are: Virgo, Capricorn, Cancer, Pisces

Her worst bets are: Scorpio, Leo, Sagittarius, Aquarius

50-50: Aries, Taurus, Gemini, Libra

THE GEMINI WOMAN *(May 21–June 20):*

How to win her: Make a mind connection with her first. She knows enough to talk about lots of things but not in-depth. She is impressed with intellectual men. She is always on the move, bouncing back and forth before she makes up her mind about you. So be patient with her. Don't get physical until you've captured her intellect. She likes to keep busy, so find her things she can do for you. Show your appreciation for her help. Compliment her intelligence and ability. She'll love it. She likes to flirt around but needs someone stable she can anchor to. She is creative, so find things that help her demonstrate it. She gets depressed easily, so be her cheerleader. She needs assurances.

How to lose her: Don't try to control her activities or restrict them, or she'll become quarrelsome and filled with anxiety. She is very independent and hates restrictions. Talk about depressing, negative subjects, and she might fall into depression. Don't tell her you really care for her, and she will lose confidence in you.

Her best bets are: Libra, Aquarius, Gemini, Pisces

Her worst bets are: Aries, Leo, Sagittarius, Capricorn

50-50: Taurus, Cancer, Virgo, Scorpio

THE CANCER WOMAN *(June 21–July 22):*

How to win her: She prefers tradition and security. She likes strong, dominant males but not oppressors. She often needs help making decisions. She likes social activities but is most attracted to family, home and children. Take an interest in these things. She can go from laughter to tears in a nanosecond. Coax her from this situation gently. Be patient and understanding. She is sympathetic to others' emotions. She may put you on a pedestal. Maintain your stature, or she'll be hurt. She needs you to be there for her, strong and steady. She is uncomfortable with outside-the-box thinking.

How to lose her: She won't like it if you show no interest in her family, friends or children in general. Don't discuss your personal affairs in public. She is careful with money and does not appreciate a spendthrift. Criticize her publicly, and she might fall to pieces.

Her best bets are: Scorpio, Pisces, Taurus, Virgo

Her worst bets are: Aries, Leo, Sagittarius, Gemini

50-50: Cancer, Libra, Capricorn, Aquarius

THE LEO WOMAN *(July 23–August 22):*

How to win her: She likes being the center of the universe, so pay attention to her. She'll let you be king as long as you let her be queen. She likes popularity, so take her out among friends often. She likes gifts and surprises that make her the centerpiece. She'll love your creativity in this area. She is a homebody at heart and will always have friends over. Support her. She is open to any conversation, so engage her in the most intimate of topics. She wants to be your friend and lover at the same time, so learn when it's best to be her friend or her lover. Be open, frank and truthful with her; she doesn't like evasiveness.

How to lose her: Criticize her friends and the way she dresses. Ask her to do something she views as demeaning. Bump her off the pedestal. Put down her family and her home. Don't make her feel like the queen in your relationship. Push your views on her. She likes her independence. Dominate her or steal her place at the center of attention, and she'll be history.

Her best bets are: Aries, Sagittarius, Leo, Aquarius

Her worst bets are: Gemini, Cancer, Pisces, Scorpio

50-50: Taurus, Virgo, Libra, Capricorn

THE VIRGO WOMAN *(August 23–September 22):*

How to win her: She wants someone with ambitions for financial success, but the money is less important than the ambition. She is practical and down-to-earth, so the gifts you give her should be practical and useful. Somewhat cool and reserved on the surface, she is passionate on the inside for the one she chooses. She sets high standards and may criticize you for failing to live up to them. She appreciates people with strong minds and intellects.

How to lose her: Don't consult her about important decisions. Emotional outbursts from you will surely turn her off. She appreciates self-control. She likes to keep secrets and will refuse to divulge them when you pressure her. She likes kindness and consideration more than material things.

Her best bets are: Taurus, Cancer, Capricorn, Pisces, Virgo

Her worst bets are: Scorpio, Aquarius, Leo, Aries

50-50: Gemini, Libra, Sagittarius

THE LIBRA WOMAN *(September 23–October 22):*

How to win her: She is a romantic and likes swashbuckling hero types. She also has a tendency to be sarcastic or cynical about things in general. She needs time to get acquainted and shrinks when you're too aggressive. Be tolerant. She likes someone with an organized pattern to his life and self-discipline, even if she herself lacks those qualities. She has a tendency to freak out over some trivial thing you do but may overlook a huge mistake. She may get angry easily but will shortly forget about it. She does a constant balancing act with her physical, emotional, spiritual and intellectual self.

How to lose her: She prefers calm and peace of mind. You can shatter this by blowing your cool all the time. Don't expect her to go camping with you unless you have a very large, very well equipped camper. She'd prefer a night at the Ritz. Avoid talking about art and theater as if you really don't like them. Cramp her style with your frugality and economy. She's a natural spender and loves shopping.

Her best bets are: Gemini, Aquarius, Leo, Aries, Virgo

Her worst bets are: Taurus, Capricorn, Scorpio, Sagittarius

50-50: Cancer, Libra, Pisces

THE SCORPIO WOMAN *(October 23–November 22):*

How to win her: This woman has a deep sexuality that she keeps secret from all but the luckiest of men. She is headstrong, aggressive and forward. She needs a man who matches her ability, independence, strength and resourcefulness in a commanding way. She needs to be the centerpiece of your thoughts, so don't take her for granted. She likes money and material success and will be patient if you have potential in those areas. If you have a future to talk about, she'll listen attentively. When she's angry, she can become acidic and loud, so thicken your skin and turn a deaf ear. She'll probably forget what she said or how angry she was within a half-hour. Watch your behavior and be discreet. She is concerned with what others think and say about her.

How to lose her: She'll hate it if you act wimpy or weak. She won't be happy if you are the least bit defeated by anything. She expects you to always appear undaunted by even the toughest situations. She doesn't like men who are peevish or vacillating or negative. It's okay for her to be caustic, cynical and abrasive, but she expects you to demonstrate cool calmness and self-control at all times.

Her best bets are: Cancer, Pisces, Capricorn, Sagittarius, Gemini

Her worst bets are: Aries, Taurus, Leo, Virgo, Libra

50-50: Scorpio, Aquarius

THE SAGITTARIUS WOMAN *(November 23–December 21):*

How to win her: She's looking for a nice guy. She wants a man who is considerate, courteous, good-hearted and charming. She's quite outspoken and occasionally forgets to think before speaking, so prepare for a few shockers. She's smart and appreciates a smart man. She's independent and capable, but she still needs a strong, dependable man to anchor herself to. She'll test you for weakness. Don't let her intimidate you. She will sometimes obsess over little things and make herself depressed. Cheer her up and offer constructive advice about her problems. She'll be especially happy if you don't flirt with other women.

How to lose her: Try bossing her around. Don't be diplomatic with her. Give her public displays of affection as she prefers men who wait until they have privacy to turn up the steam. She prefers living in civilization. Take her out to the boondocks with nothing to do, and she'll go crazy. She needs activity, especially for her mind.

Her best bets are: Aries, Leo, Scorpio, Virgo, Sagittarius

Her worst bets are: Gemini, Cancer, Libra, Taurus

50-50: Capricorn, Aquarius, Pisces

Astrologically Speaking II: East Meets West

Is your mate a Snake or a Rat? Do Dogs make loyal friends? In Chinese astrology, each of the 12 zodiac signs is characterized by a different animal. Each animal embodies the sign's most dominant traits, as seen through Eastern eyes.

To many Westerners, some Chinese zodiacal signs seem like insulting choices on which to base one's character. In the West, the Rat, for example, is commonly thought of as a dirty, destructive scavenger. The Snake is perceived as slimy, sneaky and dishonest. And the Pig is seen as filthy and slovenly. In Eastern culture, however, these same animals are greatly respected: the Rat for its ability to acquire items of value and the Pig for its superior intelligence and tenacity.

Just as each sun sign relates differently to the other signs of the zodiac, each Chinese sign interacts with others in its own special way. One key difference is that Chinese signs are also tied directly to your year of birth. The chart below was taken from SunnCity.com and displays Chinese compatibility numbers from one to 10, with 10 being most compatible:

	Rat	Ox	Tiger	Rabbit	Dragon	Snake	Horse	Goat	Monkey	Rooster	Dog	Pig
Rat	9	6	4	7	10	7	3	4	10	6	8	8
Ox	6	8	4	8	7	9	5	2	4	9	7	7
Tiger	4	4	5	5	6	3	9	4	2	4	9	7
Rabbit	7	8	5	8	7	7	5	9	4	2	8	9
Dragon	10	7	6	7	9	8	8	7	10	9	2	8
Snake	7	9	3	7	8	8	4	7	4	9	8	4
Horse	3	5	9	5	8	4	8	8	5	6	9	6
Goat	4	2	4	9	7	7	8	9	5	5	4	9
Monkey	10	4	2	4	10	4	5	5	9	4	8	7
Rooster	6	9	4	2	9	9	6	5	4	4	5	5
Dog	8	7	9	8	2	8	9	4	8	5	7	7
Pig	8	7	7	9	8	4	6	9	7	5	7	8

Keep in mind that the Chinese New Year does not coincide with our traditional January 1 New Year. The Chinese New Year may occur any time from mid-January to mid-February. If your birthday falls in that time period, check the actual date of the Chinese New Year during the year when you were born. If you don't like reading charts, here's a quick reference of your most- and least-compatible signs.

The Rat
(1900 | 1912 | 1924 | 1936 | 1948 | 1960 | 1972 | 1984)
Best bets: Rat, Rabbit, Dragon, Monkey, Dog, Pig
Worst bets: Tiger, Horse, Goat
50-50: Ox, Snake, Rooster

The Ox
(1901 | 1913 | 1925 | 1937 | 1949 | 1961 | 1973 | 1985)
Best bets: Ox, Rabbit, Dragon, Snake, Rooster, Dog, Pig
Worst bets: Tiger, Horse, Goat, Monkey
50-50: Rat

The Tiger
(1902 | 1914 | 1926 | 1938 | 1950 | 1962 | 1974 | 1986)
Best bets: Horse, Dog, Pig
Worst bets: Rat, Ox, Snake, Goat, Monkey, Rooster
50-50: Tiger, Rabbit, Dragon

The Rabbit
(1903 | 1915 | 1927 | 1939 | 1951 | 1963 | 1975 | 1987)
Best bets: Rat, Ox, Rabbit, Dragon, Snake, Goat, Dog, Pig, Horse
Worst bets: Monkey, Rooster
50-50: Tiger

The Dragon
(1904 | 1916 | 1928 | 1940 | 1952 | 1964 | 1976)
Best bets: Rat, Ox, Rabbit, Dragon, Snake, Horse, Goat, Monkey, Rooster, Pig
Worst bets: Dog
50-50: Tiger

The Snake
(1905 | 1917 | 1929 | 1941 | 1953 | 1965 | 1977)
Best bets: Rat, Ox, Rabbit, Dragon, Snake, Goat, Rooster, Dog, Horse
Worst bets: Tiger, Monkey, Pig
50-50: None

The Horse
(1906 | 1918 | 1930 | 1942 | 1954 | 1966 | 1978)
Best bets: Tiger, Dragon, Horse, Goat, Dog
Worst bets: Rat, Snake
50-50: Ox, Rabbit, Monkey, Rooster, Pig

The Goat
(1907 | 1919 | 1931 | 1943 | 1955 | 1967 | 1979)
Best bets: Rabbit, Dragon, Snake, Horse, Goat, Pig, Monkey, Rooster
Worst bets: Rat, Ox, Tiger
50-50: Dog

The Monkey
(1908 | 1920 | 1932 | 1944 | 1956 | 1968 | 1980)
Best bets: Tiger, Dragon, Horse, Goat, Dog
Worst bets: Rat, Snake
50-50: Ox, Rabbit, Monkey, Rooster, Pig

The Rooster
(1909 | 1921 | 1933 | 1945 | 1957 | 1969 | 1981)
Best bets: Ox, Dragon, Snake
Worst bets: Tiger, Rabbit, Monkey, Rooster
50-50: Rat, Horse, Goat, Dog, Pig

The Dog
(1910 | 1922 | 1934 | 1946 | 1958 | 1970 | 1982)
Best bets: Rat, Ox, Tiger, Rabbit, Snake, Horse, Monkey, Dog, Pig
Worst bets: Dragon
50-50: Goat, Rooster

The Pig
(1911 | 1923 | 1935 | 1947 | 1959 | 1971 | 1983)
Best bets: Rat, Ox, Tiger, Rabbit, Dragon, Goat, Monkey, Dog, Pig
Worst bets: None
50-50: Snake, Horse, Rooster

We also found a hybrid of Eastern and Western astrology at Sunncity.com. The hybrid formula applies Eastern Japanese thinking to Western horoscopes. Once we got past the broken English and seemingly unrelated statements in these profiles, we found them to be among the most accurate predictors of compatibility. As you read through them, think about how they apply to you. And note that the dates for each sign do not correspond to the customary dates given in Western astrology.

The Aries Woman *(December 22 – January 20)*
She likely has a long, slim face and high cheekbones. Her eyebrows may curve up slightly, and her lips are probably thin. She is taller than average.

She is sensitive, systematic, ambitious and proud. She is artistic and romantic. She thinks the world sees her through rose-colored glasses. She sees the good in people and feels hurt when they disappoint her. She handles crises better than any other sign. And once she decides to do something, nothing can stop her.

She may have a confusing mix of character traits, for there is great variety within this sign. She wants the safety and security of marriage and will avoid anything unconventional. She is stubborn but will listen to reason. Be supportive and understanding with her. Make her proud of you.

The Taurus Woman *(January 21 – February 19)*
She is a slim, moderately tall woman with a squared face, a strong jaw-line and big, round, sparkling eyes. Her hair, dress and look may be unique from anyone else. Her nature is jolly, funny, unconventional and constantly changing.

She is very patient but always needs new excitement around her. Her personality makes her an excellent politician. She also loves animals and may have many pets. Love is in her head, but freedom is in her soul. She may love you but has trouble showing it at times. She will be honest with her loved one, even if she seems distant. She fears rejection but will not show her hurt.

Money is not important to her, for it is only a means to an end. She is not the jealous type and is not one to stay close to home. You will have a difficult time keeping her home. Give her freedom and respect, instead, if you want to keep her.

The Pisces Woman *(February 20 – March 20)*

She has nice skin and small, soft hands and feet. She is all woman and probably attractive enough to be desired by many men. She may get numerous marriage proposals in her lifetime.

She also lives in a dream world. She is psychic and can often foresee what will happen next. But she is also shy and gullible – a complex character – who tends to accept men as they are without trying to change them. If you think she is a shy, innocent, fragile person who needs protection, think again. She will surprise you.

She is generous and loves love and giving gifts for all occasions. In love, she can change dramatically, from angelic softness in the beginning to witch at the end.

The Aquarius Woman *(March 21 – April 20)*

If you are the jealous type or cannot handle an independent woman, you might want to look elsewhere in the zodiac. For she is independence personified and loves her own space and her own abilities and doing things for herself.

She can make you very happy or very sorry. She displays confidence and natural leadership and might do better with a cool guy who plays just a little hard-to-get with her. She has a positive outlook and loves freedom, faith, love and being right. She has her own interests and will pursue them whether you like it or not. But she often feels alone in the world and can easily be hurt.

If she loves you, you will never be bored. She is fun, talkative and teasing. And if you ever get sick, she will care for you without question.

The Capricorn Woman *(April 21 – May 20)*

She is a tall, slim, cool and quiet woman who will take her time getting ready for a social occasion and look absolutely stunning when she's finished. She can be the perfect mother, perfect housekeeper and perfect lover all rolled into one. She has excellent control of her emotions and hides her weaknesses well.

She dislikes artificiality and fakeness, yet loves music, nature, lovely scents and well-dressed men who wear after-shave. She prefers smart men who take action and pursue their goals instead of just talking about it. If she loves you, she will help you with anything and treat you respectfully. Stay away from her if you are a lazy slob, for she values neatness, cleanliness and order.

The Gemini Woman *(May 21 – June 21)*

This is a good-looking woman with brains and imagination. She is also a collection of mixed emotions and interesting facets – a fast thinker and fast mover who can juggle several projects at once with relative ease and may speak several languages.

She is also a dreamer who can easily make you fall in love with her. She expects a lot from you and will engage you in great conversations about nearly everything. She is supportive person who wants to stay by her loved one's side as an equal and a best friend. Enjoy her quick wit and sudden mood changes for what they are. She's looking for a knight in shining armor and is never satisfied with the status quo. She likes hard work and long rests.

The Cancer Woman *(June 22 – July 23)*

One minute, she's a shy, trembling lover. The next minute, she is like glue you cannot shake away. She'll follow you home like a lonely puppy or take a long silent walk with you in perfect comfort.

She needs a brave, daring man because she lacks those qualities and has many fears and insecurities. She is not jealous but is possessive. If she loves you, she will love you completely and sacrifice everything for her love. Her happiness revolves around work and love, and she will give great care to her children.

She likes money but is not extravagant or stingy. She is likely a good saver. If you don't give her trouble, she can make you very happy.

The Leo Woman *(July 24 – August 23)*

This one really stands out in a crowd. She is tall, regal and confident and looks straight ahead while others stare at her. She follows her own style and never wears anything cheap. Her graceful carriage and charisma attract many people to her, but she is hard to know.

She is selective about the people she mingles with. If you are patient, she will eventually let you in. Just know that she will always have guys after her. She is proud and does not like being challenged or questioned. She does not like being poor, either, and will go for someone with a good career or good breeding.

Sports are her passion. If you want to date her, prepare to spend money on her. She enjoys extravagance, especially when it's about her. If you don't have much money, do something creative with her.

The Virgo Woman *(August 24 – September 23)*
Similar to the Leo woman in appearance, the Virgo woman is slim and confident with a high round forehead and unique facial structure. She probably walks fast and looks straight ahead, as if searching.

Neither possessive nor jealous, women in this sign want respect more than anything. So don't swear around her or discuss inappropriate subjects. She needs a gentleman around at all times. This woman idealizes love and won't settle for anything less than a perfect mate with perfect potential. She has a tendency to be quite critical, so only other perfectionists need apply here.

The Libra Woman *(September 24 – October 23)*
Her face is oval shaped and egg-like. She has nice, smooth skin and a good figure and takes great pains to keep her skin clean and pretty. She is good at it and will tend to look younger than her chronological age. She will dress well and always leave home looking her best.

The Libra woman is a natural flirt. She can also act like a naughty little boy and still be 100% female. She can argue for hours, but she also cares a great deal what others think of her. She will never interfere with your privacy and adapts well to almost any environment. She believes taking care of the home is a woman's job and does it well. Take it step by step with her. She appreciates a slow hand and politeness in her love interest. Go easy on her.

The Scorpio Woman *(October 24 – November 22)*

A simple woman of innocent and childlike looks who always lets you know what kind of mood she is in. She may think being a woman is a liability and might prefer to be a man, though she is really all woman. She likes power and control over others.

The Scorpio woman is adept at manipulating men without them knowing it. She will get what she wants, but what she wants is a man who will earn her respect. She can read your mind, so be careful what you think about. She loves freedom, and she's a hot lady who either loves or hates everything. There's no in-between with her.

If she loves you, it won't matter what others say. She is spoiled but allows her love to overpower her. She also has a tendency to be jealous, so don't leave any old photos or love letters around. Be on time. Play hard to get. It excites her.

The Sagittarius Woman *(November 23 – December 21)*

A tall, slim, graceful woman who walks as though she is in a beauty pageant, yet trips occasionally and covers it up well. She is self-confident and straightforward and believes in her own personal style. She is also a free spirit who does not like to stay home.

She can be clumsy, for that is her nature. But she is also a no-nonsense woman who says what's on her mind directly. If she tries to overpower you, calm her down and mimic her body language. If she respects you, she will listen to you. She has excellent taste and prefers quality over quantity. She might drive a car she cannot afford or buy clothes that are too expensive for their quality. Be straight with her, because she can also be paranoid and take things to their extremes.

PART SEVEN:

Achieve Your Ultimate Goals.

"The big difference between sex for money and sex for free is that sex for money usually costs a lot less."
— Brendan Behan, 1923-1964

Love at First Byte

Is it possible to find love on the Internet? You bet it is. Though dating sites won't give out specific information about nuptials among their paid membership, we know of many married couples who admit they met on the 'net.

It *is* possible to find your soul mate and true love in cyberspace. It might even happen when you least expect it. You may join thinking you just want potential sex partners and end up discovering the love of your life. You never know.

Your best strategy for finding love is to keep an open mind and "meet" as many women as possible. And keep in mind that, all too often, love happens when you least expect it. Sometimes, the harder you look, the more elusive it may become.

Our advice: Concentrate on meeting as many potential partners as possible. Hone your profile continually and keep searching for the right chemistry. If you want a partner for life, look for a friend first. The best relationships we know started that way. Focus on having a good time. After all, life is too short for anything else.

Don't give up.

The men who participated in a *People* magazine poll created a dating wish list that included sincerity (14%), sense of humor (11%), a good body (9%), intelligence (8%), nice eyes (8%), ambition (6%), a nice butt (5%) and a nice smile (4%). We defy anyone to explain the logic behind these figures. The remaining 35% included hundreds of other wishes, none of which comprised even 1%.

The women, as you might expect, were a bit less physical when they listed sense of humor (25%), sincerity (13%), nice eyes (9%), nice smile (8%), good body (7%), intelligence (5%), height (4%), ambition (4%) and a nice butt (1%). If these sta tistics are accurate, stand-up comics must be scoring like crazy. If you are a sincere funny guy with nice eyes, you will be the envy of your male friends. You'll be the object of desire for many women, too.

We found it interesting that men value intelligent women more than women value intelligent men. We were also amused to find an attractive caboose on both male and female wish lists. Whatever happened to breasts or legs?

 **HOT TIP NUMBER 16** – *DO keep an open mind and "meet" as many women as possible if you're looking for love. And remember that, all too often, love happens when you least expect it.*

Is Anyone Really Having Sex on the Internet?

During our research for this book, we interviewed hundreds of men and women from various Internet dating sites to get a feel for what's really going on out there. Are people really "hooking up" regularly? Does Internet dating lead to more frequent sex? Exactly how common is casual sex among Internet daters?

We found a surprising number of men who were seriously looking for Ms. Right. These marriage-minded men have far more discriminating tastes and are far less likely to accept a woman's sexual advances than you would imagine. Many resist casual sex completely. They are not the dogs many women or the popular media think they are.

For many men over 40 and 50, sex is not the driving force it was when we were in our 20s and 30s. Testosterone levels begin dropping in males after age 40. When you add ingredients such as stress, obesity, lack of sleep, poor circulation, smoking and drinking, you get an effective, libido-killing cocktail.

Don't assume that everyone else is having a great time and you're not. The fact is, some men and women look for casual sex and many more don't. We believe the vast majority of men and women are looking for something more meaningful and more lasting. The tremendous popularity of reality-based TV shows such as *The Bachelor*, *Joe Millionaire*, *Married by America* and *The Bachelorette* offer sufficient evidence that love and marriage are still the gold standard in the world of desirable relationships.

But if it's sex you're after, then go to AdultFriendFinder.com. With about 15,000 new members joining every day, you'll find many choices here. If you're really open-minded, consider joining an Internet swingers group. Here you'll find a veritable smorgasbord of sexual possibilities. Just about anything goes.

For guys who want to live the American dream according to *Playboy* magazine founder and pop culture icon Hugh Hefner, adult sites are the way to go. If you think you're too old for that level of debauchery, consider the fact that Mr. Hefner turned 77 in 2003 and still parties *every night*. And he has at least six "steady" girlfriends.

Hef is still living his own dream thanks to Viagra and staying extremely active. Let that be a lesson for you.

HOT TIP NUMBER 17 – *DON'T assume that everyone else is having a great time and you're not. The fact is, some men and women look for casual sex and many more simply don't.*

PART EIGHT:

The Ultimate in Speed and Efficiency.

*"There is one who kisses,
and the other who offers the cheek."*
— French Proverb

From Cyberspace to Your Place in Three Days

If you don't think this is possible, then you don't know Internet dating. Not only is it possible, it's fairly common to meet someone within three days of the first contact. Your first contact will come via email. Some women will tell you half their life story, and some will say next to nothing. Most will include their profiles or links to their profiles within the email.

This part always reminded us of opening Christmas presents. We never knew what we'd find inside. It was always a surprise. Sometimes, it was a pleasant surprise. Sometimes, not so pleasant.

If you like the profile and picture, you can open up an email dialogue. If that goes well, you might exchange personal email addresses (most of the big dating sites mask your real email address for your protection). Or you might opt for the instant messaging route, first. Then exchange phone numbers. If your email and/or instant messaging adventures turn out well, you will swap phone numbers during the second or third exchange.

The first phone call is like opening yet another Christmas present. You've likely already seen the face. Now you get to hear the voice. If you like the voice and the call goes smoothly (no awkward moments, thoughts of "what the hell is she talking about?" or pained silences), you'll probably want a face-to-face meeting.

No matter how well the phone call goes, the first meeting should have a time limit. Many of our first meetings lasted about an hour. Some were as short as 15 minutes, while others lasted up to two hours. But there's really no rule. Do whatever makes you most comfortable. Just remember to give yourself (and her) an escape route. Tell her you only have a half-hour between business meetings. Tell her you have an appointment with your accountant, dentist or a client. You can always "cancel" the meeting if your Internet meeting heats up faster than you expected.

For the ultimate man, the first meeting should be over a drink or a cup of coffee or tea. You'll want to limit your financial exposure just as you limit your time. If all goes well, you can always change course in midstream. Some dates will offer to pay for their drinks. The ultimate man will decide whether he wants her to do that or not. Our take was that most women who do this are testing us to see whether we have a) the money to pay and b) the manners to pay. And others just prefer to remain independent until a deeper connection is established.

If the initial meeting goes well, your next step will be the first date. What you do on your first date is wide open. Your only constraints are time and money. If your initial chemistry is really good (you're thinking about her, already), plan something that will give you a chance to get to know her better. Don't take her to a movie. Sitting in silence for two hours won't tell you much about her.

No matter what you do together, one simple fact remains: You could easily be enjoying a first date with someone you didn't know existed three days ago.

If you've been dating around or just got out of a relationship or you're meeting lots of women, remember to turn all your phones off when you're with "her." We learned the hard way when one of us was home on a promising date with a promising suitor. The phone rang after midnight (strike one), an ex-girlfriend left a message (strike two) and the words "...love you" were audible (strike three).

Date over. Promising romance over. Game over.

Turn your phone off. Turn your answering machine off. Turn your cell phone off. Remember that, even though you thought you made it clear that your previous relationship was over, it might not be over as far as your ex is concerned.

Don't keep pictures of other women out in your home or apartment, either. We haven't met too many women who enjoy sharing their men with other women. If the relationship is over, get rid of the evidence.

 **HOT TIP NUMBER 18** – *DO consider staying offline until you've made a decision about her, if you're corresponding steadily with an interesting prospect. After all, if she's interested in you, she's gonna be watching YOUR online activity, too.*

By now, you should be quite comfortable with Internet dating. From your honest self-assessment at the beginning of the process to finding the right dating site to setting up your profile and knowing how to use email and various search functions to find the woman who is just right for you, you are now ready to take the plunge. We've given you all the tools and advice you need to make your Internet dating experience a raging success. The rest is up to you, the ultimate man.

You can do it. So go for it!

APPENDIX

THE ULTIMATE MAN'S GUIDE™ TO INTERNET DATING SITES

AsianDate.com
AmericanSingles.com
CoupleMakers.com
DreamDates.com
eHarmony.com
iMatchup.com
Jdate.com, for Jewish singles
Kiss.com
Match.com
Matchmaker.com
One2OneMatchmaker.com
SharedVision.com
shipmatedates.com
SinglesLibrary.com
Udate.com
YahooPersonals.com

ADULT DATING SITES

AdultFriendFinder.com is part of the Friend Finder Personals Network, which now has over 20,000,000 registered members worldwide, making it the largest personals network on the planet! Other Friend Finder Personals Network sites include the following:

AdultFriendFinder.com – Erotic personals
alt.com – BDSM/fetish personals
Amigos.com – Spanish/Portuguese personals
AsiaFriendFinder.com – Chinese personals

BigChurch.com – Religious personals
FilipinoFriendFinder.com – Filipino personals
FrenchFriendFinder.com – French personals
FriendFinder.com – Dating personals
GermanFriendFinder.com – German personals
KoreanFriendFinder.com – Korean personals
OutPersonals.com – Gay personals
SeniorFriendFinder.com – 50+ personals

MAIL-ORDER BRIDE SITES
CherryBlossoms.com
RussianLadies.com

Who Is Howard Brian Edgar, Jr.?

Howard Brian Edgar was born in New York City's Harlem district. He received his bachelor's degree in English and Fine Arts from Clemson University, Clemson, SC, where novelists Mark Steadman and H. Barry Hannah were his mentors.

He has earned his living almost exclusively as a writer since 1975, when he began as a copywriter with a Madison Avenue ad agency. Later, he wrote weekly opinion columns and covered health, politics, crime, medical and environmental issues as an investigative reporter and columnist for two Florida newspapers.

From there, Howard joined the corporate world as a senior writer and video producer for a medical rehabilitation, physical therapy and fitness equipment manufacturer. During this time, he wrote extensively about health and fitness-related issues for physicians and physical therapists, including Pat Croce, who owned the Philadelphia 76ers of the NBA and the Philadelphia Flyers of the NHL, and now appears regularly on TV as a color commentator and sports personality.

More recently, Howard has been a sports writer and worked as the creative director and senior medical writer for the nation's leading medical marketing firm. He has also won over 50 creative, inspirational and leadership awards, including Writer's Digest awards for screenwriting and short-story writing.

A combination of personal and journalistic curiosity led him to spend the past few years researching the Internet dating phenomenon from the inside. He used several online and offline dating services, scanned thousands of profiles, dated hundreds of women and interviewed hundreds more in preparation for this book. During that process, he also met someone very special to him.

Who Is Howard Martin Edgar II?

Howard Martin Edgar was born and raised as an only child by his mother and grandmother in Southern California. He received his master's degree from the School of Hard Knocks, where his mentors and influences included Mark Victor Hansen, Anthony Robbins, John Wooden, Pat Riley, W. Clement Stone and Brian Tracy.

When Howie was 18, the U.S. Navy told him that he had an aptitude for journalism. But Howie had too much energy to sit at a desk. Instead, he moved to Laguna Beach at age 21 and took a job with the local water district. Howie took a second job at night as a bouncer for several local nightclubs, learned a lot about the singles scene and dated hundreds of women in just a few years.

After a car accident forced him to leave the water district, he embarked on a sales career. His natural sales ability led him to a career as sales manager for three multimillion-dollar organizations. Howie ran the West Coast operation for a publishing company owned by the Washington Post. He also founded and operated a successful catering business during this time.

Never married, but always busy, Howie more recently joined several Internet dating sites to find and meet women. He "met" thousands of women via their Internet profiles and hundreds more face-to-face.

Howie resides in Orange County, California, and swears he always will.

And by the way, Howie is not related to co-author Howard Brian Edgar, Jr.

Other Titles That May Interest You

If you have other stories that might better fit The Ultimate Man's Guide™ titles below, send them to us. If we use your submission, we'll send you an autographed copy of the book and an opportunity to purchase additional copies at reduced prices for your friends, family, coworkers and loved ones.

Or if you'd like to make a larger contribution and become the lead writer on one of our books, we offer a lucrative profit participation package for professional writers. You might even have your own book idea that fits our model. Otherwise, you can earn by-lines for the following titles:

The Ultimate Man's Guide™ to Surviving Divorce
The Ultimate Man's Guide™ to Simple Home Cooking
The Ultimate Man's Guide™ to Survival
The Ultimate Man's Guide™ to Health & Fitness
The Ultimate Man's Guide™ to Looking & Feeling Better
The Ultimate Man's Guide™ to Having More Fun
The Ultimate Man's Guide™ to Home Improvement
The Ultimate Man's Guide™ to Office Politics
The Ultimate Man's Guide™ to Career Options
The Ultimate Man's Guide™ to Great Sex
The Ultimate Man's Guide™ to Romance
The Ultimate Man's Guide™ to Having a Baby
The Ultimate Man's Guide™ to Single Parenting
The Ultimate Man's Guide™ to Parenting
The Ultimate Man's Guide™ to Communicating With Women
The Ultimate Man's Guide™ to Caring for Aging Parents
The Ultimate Man's Guide™ to Sports Legends
The Ultimate Man's Guide™ to Smart Money Management

The Ultimate Man's Guide™ to War Stories
The Ultimate Man's Guide™ to Home Entertainment
The Ultimate Man's Guide™ to Adventure Travel
The Ultimate Man's Guide™ to Cheap Vacations
The Ultimate Man's Guide™ to Great Vacations
The Ultimate Man's Guide™ to Spirits & Smokes
The Ultimate Man's Guide™ to Getting the Most Out of Life
The Ultimate Man's Guide™ to Success Beyond Your Dreams

And Now... It's Your Turn!

We want to hear all about your Internet dating experiences. In fact, we want to put you in our next book, *The Ultimate Man's Guide™ to True Internet Dating Stories.*

Did you meet your wife on the Internet? How? What was your best date like? What was your worst date like? We want to hear it all. Tell us the good, the bad and the ugly. Tell us about your hottest sexual encounter. Or your most embarrassing moment. Or your greatest Internet dating discovery.

If you have ever wanted to see your name in print, this is your chance. Your by-line will appear with your story (unless you prefer to remain anonymous). And if we do use your submission, you will receive an autographed free copy of the book as a token of our appreciation. You'll receive all that plus a chance to purchase additional copies at reduced prices for friends, family, coworkers and loved ones.

If you believe in the notion that everyone is entitled to 15 minutes of fame, this is your chance to grab yours. And all you have to do is send us your true story via email or snail mail.

Our email address is: stories@theultimatemansguide.com

Our snail mail address is: H² Productions, 26895 Aliso Creek Road, Suite B483, Aliso Viejo, CA 92656. And be sure to include your name, age, email address and/or snail mail address with your submission. Submissions can be any length.

We look forward to hearing from you.

Look for The Ultimate Man's Gear at:
www.theultimatemansguide.com